As A Shaman Dreams

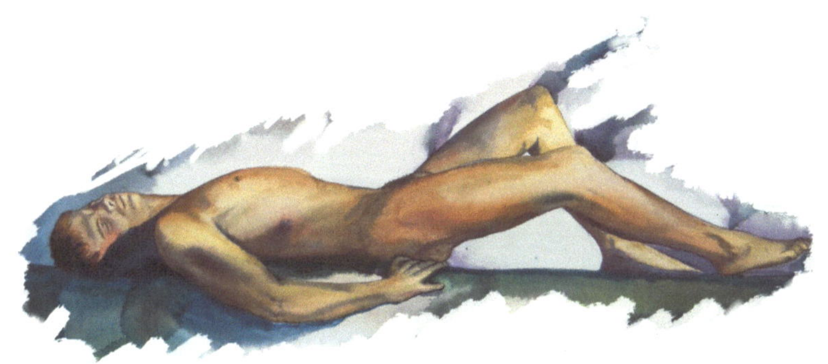

by Gene Stirm

ISBN-13: 978-0-9826828-2-1

First Edition
First Printing September, 2011

Published by:
Way West Productions
1220 Alder Avenue
Tehachapi, CA 93561

Dedication

To Patricia and my girls; Malinda, Ashlynn, Karissa, Elizabeth and Bethany.

Acknowledgements

Special thanks to Patricia Stirm, my wise and lovely wife, who's encouragement, support and faith brought me to this creation.

Gratefulness is expressed to J. Kenneth Pringle, Alexander (Sandy) Rogers, David S. Whitley and the staffs of Eastern California Museum, Independence, CA and Maturango Museum, Ridgecrest, CA.

Gratitude is also extended to the many people that have done so much to bring the understanding of Shamanism to a modern world, including , but surely not limited to; Michael Harner, Roger Walsh, Arnold Mindell, Jill Kuykendall and Hank Wesselman.

Lastly, I wish to thank Ashlynn Leete and Eugenio (Kenney) Tapia, my extra set of eyes.

Foreword

There is a striking similarity in Shaman rock art world wide. Though the art was created by many different peoples using simple stone tools, primitive to our standards, on various surfaces, it all comes from the same creative human minds, and though the art may date back thousand of years the human mind that created it was certainly not primitive. The art they created is as contemporary as the art that hangs in modern museums or the graphic design work done on the latest computers. People today often grossly underestimate the creative mind and genius of the people some term as primitive.

When the manuscript for this book was finished and moving into the design stage, National Geographic published an article entitled. 'The Birth of Religion, The World's First Temple', June, 2011, VOL. 219, NO. 6. The stunning similarities of the 11,600 year old art from southern Turkey, to the petroglyphs of the American southwest Great Basin, were amazing, but not surprising, simply a further demonstration of the universality of Shaman art. With due respect to National Geographic, in my opinion, Turkey, is not the birthplace of religion, nor is the temple of Göbekli Tepe in southern Turkey, the worlds first temple, those secrets are yet to be discovered.

Shaman art from around the globe is very similar and if the photographs or drawings are not identified, their original locations are sometimes difficult to identify. Shaman art is universal and as I studied Shamanism's concepts and beliefs, I found them just as universal. Shamanism is the foundation and forerunner of all religions in the world, past and present. In this work I have tried to relate these concepts and beliefs to photographs of the Shaman art from the southwest Great Basin of the United States, from a contemporary Shaman's perspective.

GENE

About the Author

Gene Stirm fell in love with the arts at an early age. In high school he was active in art and theater. Winning honors in display design and stage design, including the Bank of America Award for Fine Art. After two years of college and a number of personal and family conflicts, he chose to move to the mountains near Yosemite, which turned into a year long quest for self, his very special Vision Quest. After finding himself, he figured he wasn't really lost, and refocused his direction towards commercial art and graphic design. Finishing art school in 1971, he went to work for a weekly newspaper and commercial printing company in Central California. With the knowledge of printing now reinforcing his graphic arts and design skills, he took a position as a studio artist at a full-service advertising agency. There, he participated in everything from typesetting, illustrations and photography to storyboarding, copywriting and even directing commercials for TV. He was then hired as art director for Josten's American Yearbook Company, in Visalia, California where he continued studying book design and photography, including studying with Ansel Adams, even guest lectured at the Ansel Adams Workshops in Yosemite.

He moved to Orange County, California, in the late 1970's, and after managing two printing companies, doors opened in the area of menu design where he combined his restaurateur knowledge with his art training and cover design experience. His work was in demand and he and a partner started Stirm/Collins & Associates, a menu design company with a client list that included; The Fairmont Corporation, The Plaza, NY; The Beverly Wilshire, The Bel Air and Halekulani. Along the way, he completed seminary studies, was ordained and pastored a non-denominational church for ten years.

In 2004, he and his wife moved to Tehachapi, California, where he continued his studies of Native American art and culture and Shamanism. In 2008, he received a Doctor of Shamanism Degree, from ULC Seminary.

Gene has been connected with photography, publishing, book design and writing most of his professional life. His writing credits include: Editor of Impression, Josten's employee magazine; writer and editor, OC Orchid Society Bulletin, a photographic book, *O Israel, Is Your Fig Tree Budding;* the novel, *Mystical Path To Mystique,* published 2010; *The Art and Craft of Cover Design, published 2010.* He also co-authored the photographic book, *Oscar Goes Camping,* with Chelley Kitzmiller in 2011.

Content

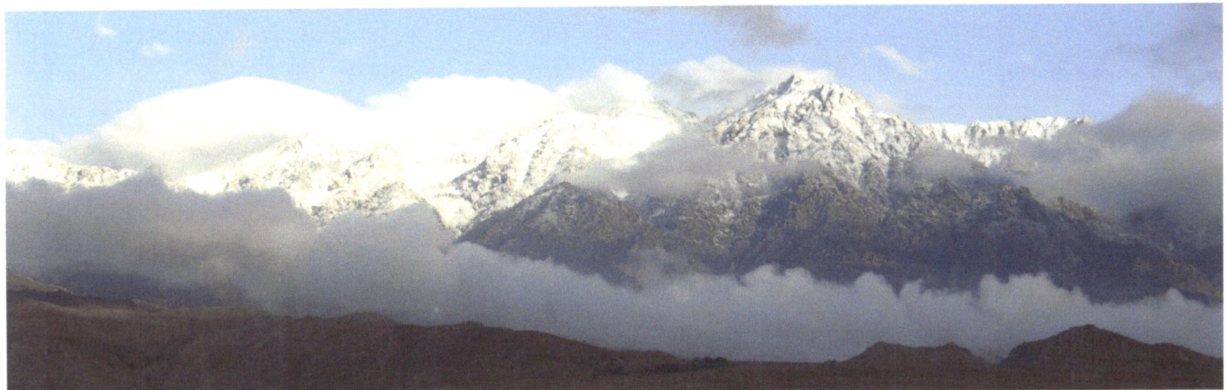

Easter Sierra Mountains, Fort Independents Indian Reservation, California.

Introduction

Shamanism is the world's oldest spiritual belief system. Before writing, before religious and dogmas, before priests, there were Shamans. The Shamans were the spiritual advisers, healers and sometimes head or leader of their clan. Shamans had the knowledge to use healing herbs, dress wounds, set broken bones, heal the sick and work, for want of a better word, magic. Shamans saw beyond the ordinary, dealt with spiritual matter and taught the people about their origin, their God and their purpose in life. They taught by myths and parables from knowledge received by Mystical Journeys to the Spirit World.

Shamans received a call from the Great Spirit, Devine Wisdom, God. Once accepting the call, they faced the ordeal of the Vision Quest, a personal time of introspection and initiation. Then, by mentors and by Spirit Guides, both human and animal, they learned the ways of the Shaman. Shamanism is always a firsthand experience. One must experience the process of death to self and rebirth of the human spirit to become a Shaman. Though the methods may vary, the process is universally similar.

In the middle of the last century, a spiritual awaking moved across the Earth, awaking old ideas and spawning new beliefs. One of these reemerging practices was Shamanism, brought back to the modern world by anthropologies and explorers from the primitive corners of the Earth. Fuelled by Carlos Castaneda's writings and new psychedelic drugs, it was at first dismissed as another movement of the sixties. But the seed once planted, germinated and began to grow in individuals and small groups around the world.

Contemporary Shamanism owes a good deal of its growth and acceptance to the work of anthropologist Michael Harner, Ph.D. He discovered a method of Journeying, entering an altered state of consciousness, without the use of hallucinatory drugs. His technique uses drumming and other rhythmic instruments. Additional techniques of self-hypnosis allow altered state of consciousness, again without the use of hallucinogenic drugs.

Beliefs

Shamans generally believe that the Earth is a spirit world. That everything has a spirit or energy. They also profess that the Earth has at least three levels or worlds. These worlds are subdivided by some into layers of seven and further multiples of seven. The three worlds consist of the middle, lower and upper world, and are joined by the Tree of Life. These worlds are not the same as Christians' Earth, heaven and hell, they are spiritual worlds .

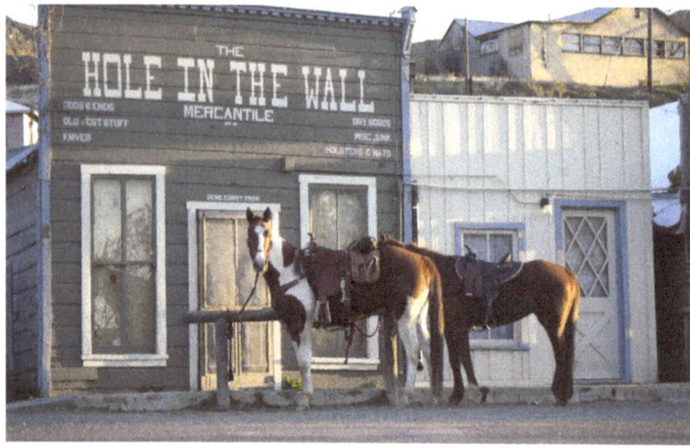

Middle world. Ransburg, CA, a living ghost town.

Middle World

The middle world is where humans dwell. Physical laws of, time, gravity, birth and death govern this world. This is the realm of evil, death and decay. The middle world is a land of toil and struggle, where humans struggle and learn the lessons of life. It is believed that humans live many lifetimes in the middle world before moving permanently to a higher spiritual realm, the other side, heaven, this is not the same as the upper word.

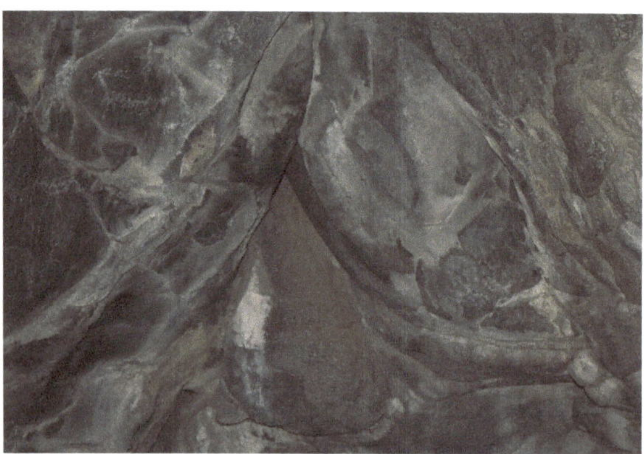

Portal to the lower world,
Little Petroglyph Canyon, Ridgecrest, CA.

Lower World

The lower world is a place of nurturing, Mother Earth, the womb of middle Earth. It is not a world of evil, pain, torment and devils, a relative new concept developed by modern religions. Shamans believe the lower world, though inhabited by strange beings of bizarre shapes and sizes, is a benevolent place.

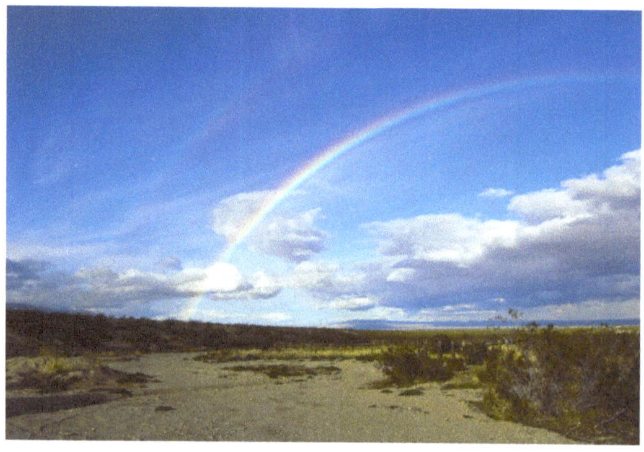

Upper world, after a thunderstorm in the Mojave Desert, CA.

Upper World

For the Shaman, the upper world is the realm of the seeker, the place of wisdom and knowledge. It is the abode of the spirits of the four winds, rain and Father Sky. The upper and lower worlds exist near parallel with the middle world, just slightly above or below the middle world similar to quantum physics parallel universes theory. Shaman, through the method of Journeying can enter these worlds to help their people with healing, finding food, shelter, protection and wisdom gained from the Universal Mind of God, whom humans will someday reunite and become once again, one.

The Journey Begins

The late summer morning promised to be hot. A steady easterly breeze blew from the Mojave Desert. I stepped to my studio, my sanctuary, a small room detached from the house. I built it the first summer after we moved to Tehachapi. A window faced north, through which I can see the southern end of the Sierra Mountains. In a valley between, partly obscured by trees, a sleepy village reluctantly stirred to life. Thin shafts of sunlight filter through the curtained windows of the east-facing door.

I anticipated this day ever since the idea for this book first came to me. Two months ago, it flashed into my head. Suddenly in my mind's eye, I saw it, so real I could touch the pages, see the photographs and read the words. I immediately went to my office and made notes. The size, approximant number of pages, photographs, and title was clear, the book, *As a Shaman Dreams*, a photographic book about petroglyphs interpreted through the spiritual journeying of a Shaman.

When the euphoria had passed, the scope of such a project hit me. A forty-year career as a graphic artist gave me the artist perspective. And I had practiced Shamanism for several years, but up until now primarily in private. Was I ready to open myself to the possible ridicule such an undertaking could bring? To accomplish this work, I would have to expose my ideas, philosophy and methods. Was I ready?

I took a deep breath, expelled it slowly and claiming myself. In the east corner of the room, a small altar was ready. On top of a hand-woven red and black mat sat a large glass bowl filled with local desert sand, and in the center, a blue candle. I lit it, and in turn lit smudges of sweet grass, sage and native tobacco, my simple offering. Next, I took a rawhide rattle and shook a constant rhythm, acknowledged the four directs of the compass, Father Sky above and Mother Earth below and then returned it to its place. Grounded and ready, I sat in my chair and prepared to Journey. I use a blend of meditation and self-hypnosis. I have never used or experimented with hallucinatory drugs that became a popular part of the Shaman revival of the 1960's. It took thirty years for me to develop my own methods of Journeying by reaching an Altered State of Consciousness, ASC.

Relaxing in my chair I used self-hypnosis, and entered a state of ASC. I gave myself intent, to visit the lower world and seek clarification, direction, style and content of this book. I began by envisioning a descent down a twenty-one step staircase. At the foot of the stairs, I peered into the darkness. At last I saw a canyon wall and in it the hollow that would lead me to my destination, the lower world.

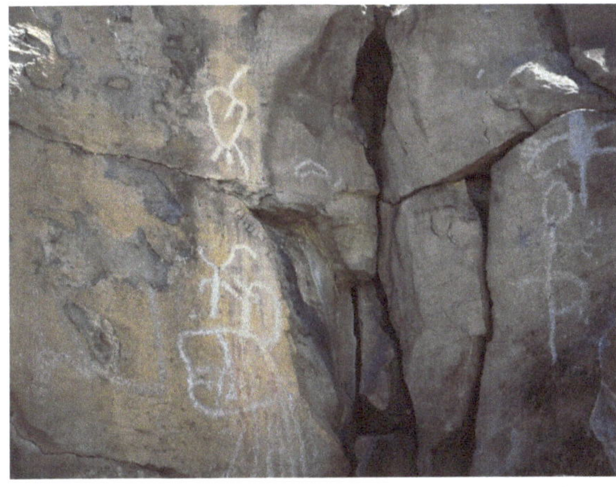

Shaman portal to lower world, Little Petroglyph Canyon, CA.

I had felt the hard stone before. My fingers explored until they found the crack, the thin fracture in the stone, the door. The stone was warm to the touch. My heart quickened as I wondered if I was worthy and the gatekeeper would grant me entry. Slowly the stone softened and Mother Earth opened herself. I entered her womb. Warm, secure and comforted, I drifted in darkness until abstract phantasmagorias began to appear all about me. I danced with the images until at last I became part of them. The living, breathing book I was to bring forth.

This Book

I was the art director of a large publishing company when first introduced to petroglyph and pictograph of Southern California in 1974, while doing the layout of a book for the San Bernardino County Museum. Since that introduction I have been a collector of, drawings, photographs and examples of Native American art and similar aboriginal art from around the world. Source material that I have often used in my art career.

I have also had a great interest in all things spiritual which lead to seminary studies. After graduate and ordination to the minister, I pastored for ten years. Twenty years ago as my two passions began to merge, the love of Native American art and ministry, I began an intense study of Shamanism, first in the Americas and then worldwide Shamanism.

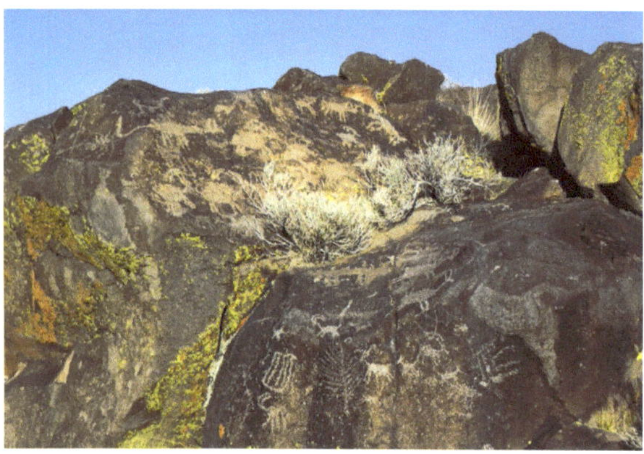

Little Petroglyph Canyon, Ridgecrest, CA

In 2005, I made my first trip to photograph Little Petroglyph Canyon near Ridgecrest, California. An anthropologist known as an authority on the area's petroglyph accompanied me. Stunned and reverenced by the magnitude of the art in this magnificent canyon, I wept. However, with all my guides' knowledge of the people who created the art, he lacked understanding of the meaning of the art itself. I began photographing the area's petroglyphs for my own collection. At that time, I came across the writings of David Whitley, Ph.D. He believes the images were of Shamanistic in meaning, which my spirit and intellect agreed.

A Shaman's Perspective

The photographs in this book where selected from the thousands of images I have made over the past six years. The only manipulations of the images are cropping, contrast and preparation for printing. However, there are a small group of images masked, layered and interspersed with photograph and drawings of real people. I then used a computer and Photoshop® to generate my own, dreamlike works of art, I call, Shaman Dreams, which is clearly evident and noted in this work. All Shaman art in this book is genuine, photographed by me on location using Nikon cameras and lens.

The interpretations and commentaries in this book are my own. Building on the belief that the art was Shaman made images inspired by Shaman Journeying to the spirit realm through altered states of consciousness, I choose a group from my collection of photographs representing the areas of Southern California and Nevada. Taking one print at a time, I entered a trance state and Journeyed to the other worlds of the Shaman, seeking interpretation and meaning.

I am not a scientist or anthropologist and this work in no way claims to be authoritative as such. I do bring to this work a lifetime of both artistic and spiritual pursuits, and while influenced by my location and contact with local Native Americans, I do not pretend to be Native American. My beliefs in and practice of Shamanism, are not connected to any ethnic group or culture, but is the sum of studies of Shamanism as practiced universally and my own first hand experience. The intention of this work is as an inspirational artistic effort, meant to foster a deeper appreciation of the gifts the Ancient Ones left us.

Paka

My granddaughter gave me the name Paka, which means 'wind' or 'spirit' in the Paiute language, as in pakagunt, meaning 'man having power' or 'Shaman.' I embrace Shamanism not as a religion, but as a holistic worldview. I simply practice and share what I have learned and experienced first-hand. I believe in the old adage, 'practice what you preach.' I am not an Old World, Asian nor Native American Shaman; I practice what I call, Contemporary American Shamanism.

I want to reiterate that Shamanism is based on firsthand spiritual experiences, and while there any number of books on the subject, they can only point the direction and give you hints to find your way, they cannot make you a Shaman. The same is true for workshop and seminars, no two Shaman walk the same path.

Before The Dreams

Do not fear for I come in peace. If you will dare walk with me awhile I will share with you what I see and what I hear when I dream.

They call me Paka, Spirit Wind. My people are all the people of the Earth. I come silently, stand patiently and wait to be invited to speak. You have heard my voice in the wind and seen my face in the clouds. I hold in my left hand three sticks, knowledge, wisdom and power. In my right hand, I hold the medicine bundle to heal the nations.

I am a dreamer, a Shaman. I dream special dreams. In a state between awake and sleep I see other places and other worlds. Some are exactly like your own and others strange beyond description, such that I can only show you with the marks I make on paper. Like those that have come before me and made their marks on the rock walls of the Sacred Places', canyons, caves and special stones. I leave this book for you.

The Call

I first began to dream when I was a young and sickly. The medicine men of the day said my heart was weak, my blood was boiling, my mind had no direction and I was depressed and lost and would die soon. They gave me foul tasting pills and took my blood to make many tests. Their medicine made me have terrible nightmares. Finally, one wise doctor said I should make a Vision Quest. I knew the medicine the other white-coats were giving me would surely kill me. My family feared and my friends lamented, but I took my leave.

Alone, I went to a valley in the mountains of California called Yosemite. In the early spring, I shivered in the cold as I made my camp. By summer, my heart was strong and I threw away the fowl medicine. With the breeze, I hiked the high country. Father sky and Mother Earth my only friends kept me safe and under the starry sky, I began to dream new dreams. I found my Quest.

When the first snows came again, I returned home. Only I had no home, and old friend no longer knew me. I was like the wind, felt but not seen.

Many winters have come and gone since that time, I have grown old, a little wiser and learned the way of the Shaman. Many paths have passed beneath my feet. Some good and some not, but always, I have learned. Come, walk with me awhile, I will share with you what I see and what I hear when I dream.

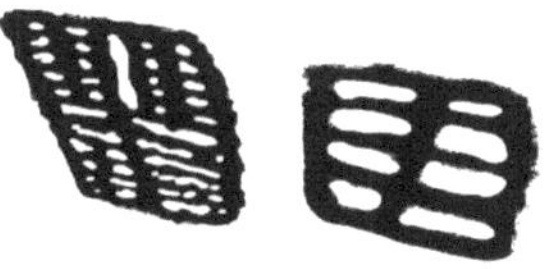

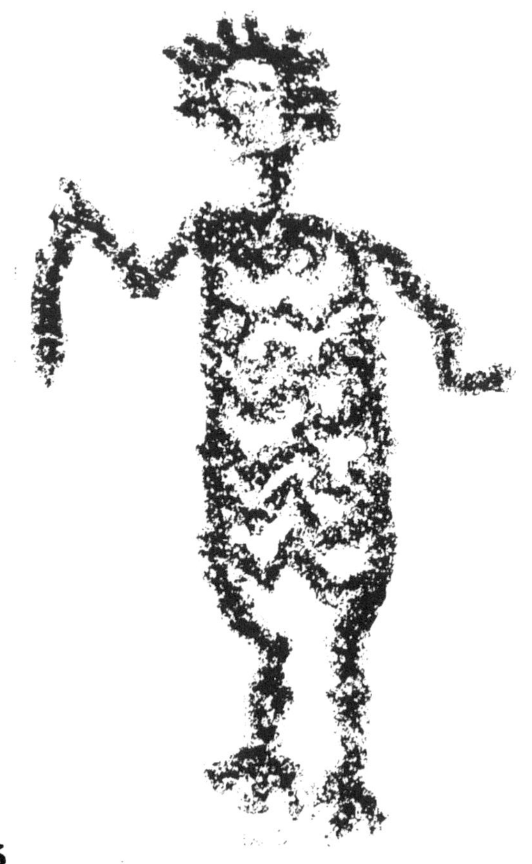

The Dream Begins

I come to my special place. A place of quiet, sheltered from the, out there world. Near the entrance, I kindle a small flame on the altar. White smoke from sage and sweet grass rise and with a feather, I call the smudge to me. It surrounds me. I make an offering of wild tobacco to the four winds, Father Sky and Mother Earth. Wrapped in the cloak of the smoke, I make myself ready for the journey. I am prepared.

In the center of this special space, I sit comfortably and tell my body to relax. Intentionally I shed all that connects me to the now world and strip away all the binds. The drum begins to beat, my horse that will take me to the worlds of spirits. I speak to my body, telling it to let go of the now world and I feel it respond. Soon the walls begin to expand and a warm sensation of freedom washes over me. There is darkness all around, warm, pleasant emptiness that is safe and sheltering. I drift.

The drum and my heart are of one beat. In the dark, lights begin to move and pulsate. Images of thing known and strange commence to dance with me. Round and round we go until we lift high in the air and Earth, like a moon, shines in the night sky. I journey.

At last, the festival of light and dancing shapes and creatures have carried me to the other worlds. In the meadow, beneath the Earth moon I lie down at the foot of the Tree of Life and fall into a special sleep. I dream.

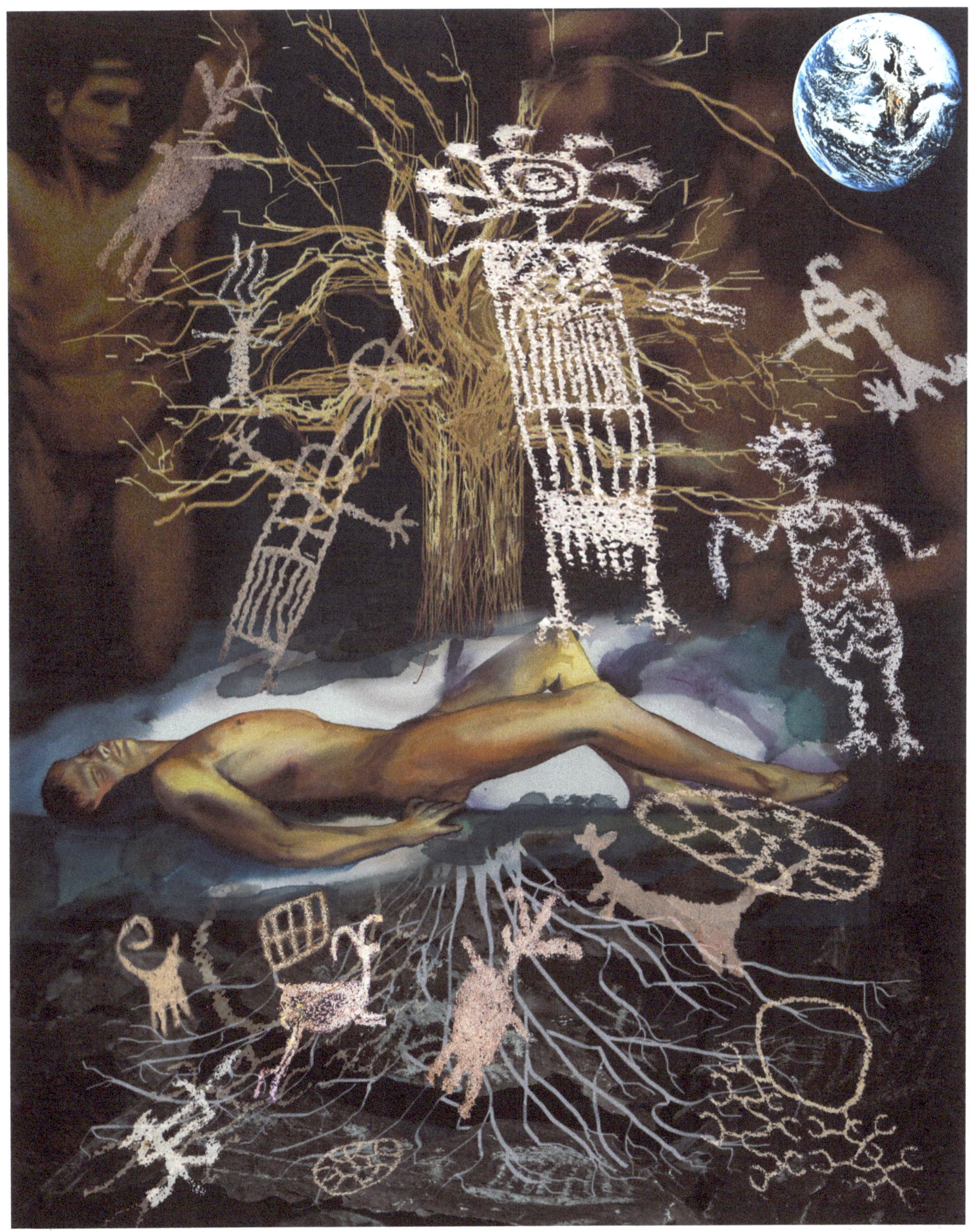

The Dream Begins Montage — A Shaman lies dreaming beneath the Tree of Life, guarded by Shaman spirits, helpers and guides.

Rite of Passage

An ancient Book of Wisdom says, "For a lack of vision the people parish." Finding and defining one's vision, purpose in life, is essential for a happy productive life. Without a vision, we wander in a spiritual desert seeking pleasure from external sources, never satisfied, never fulfilled, never finding bliss.

There comes a time in every child's life when he or she must put away childish things and assume the role of an adult. In some cultures and families this rite of passage rituals are defined by, first communion, bar mitzvah or bat mitzvah, shinbyu, or identifiable markers. For others, this rite is lost to the needs of working parents, television-babysitters and street gangs. To the early people of North America, the vision quest was a prominent part of the ritual of becoming an adult. Today, many confuse or combine the rite of passage and vision quests, believing they are the same.

North American traditions, vary by region and tribe, but overall are very similar. The initiate would separate his or her self from all human contact, and without weapon or substance find a secluded location, and according to their tribal practice, mark the space as sacred. Alone, hungry and exposed to the elements, playing a repetitious rhythm instrument, chanting, repeated prayer or by administrating drugs the seeker would enter an Altered State of Consciousness. It was during this ASC that the seeker would receive their vision.

When the seeker returned home or normal life, they would commemorate the experience. In the case of a vision quest in connection with a rite of passage, there was usually a sacred place, stone or cave where the initiate made a mark signifying their vision. This mark could be anything from a handprint to an elaborate stone pecked engraving. In some cultures the ritual would be marked on the body with tattoos, scaring or circumcision.

Girls rite of passage was established by their first menstrual cycle and instead of going into the wilderness would be confined in a shelter or cave for several days.

The Vision Quest

The vision quest is not solely a part of the rite of passage, nor only a Shaman practice. A vision quest is a formal stepping aside from normal daily life for the purpose of clarification of direction through supernatural means. Direction may come from the Universal Mind, God, spirit beings, spirit guides or spirit animal guides. Most religions of old had a form of vision quest or seeking supernatural spiritual guidance, however, in today's world, spiritual studies and rites of passage are no more complex than joining a church, organization, or a long night out on the town with one's buddies on a twenty-first birthday.

A vision quest begins with a declaration of intent, the defining of information sought. After the declaration, there is a separation from the ordinary and a seeking of a meditative state. The vision or guidance may come quickly or only after much fasting and prayer in isolation, depending on how intuitive the petitioner is to the spirit world. A person may wander forty days and nights in the wilderness seeking direction or spend a single night of earnest prayer in a garden in order to find an answer. Neither are vision quest's limited to a, once in a lifetime experience, but can be sought anytime there is a need for direction.

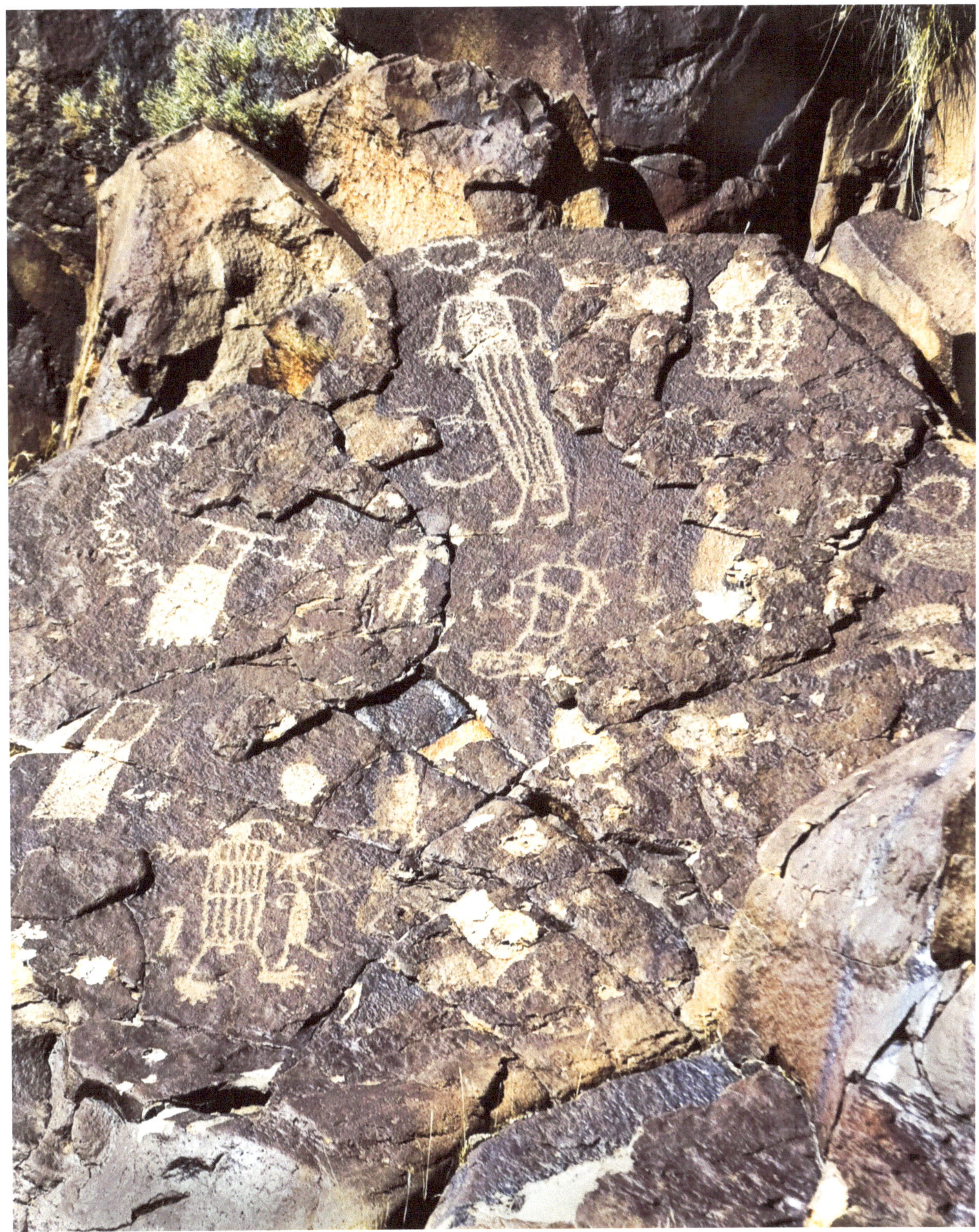

Some petroglyphs were make by the initiate to commemorate a Rite of Passage or Vision Quest after their ritual.

The Seeker

I walk in a high place today and marvel at what I see. I see so much I do not understand. There is such a thick veil between the spirit world and me. In my head, I know I have chosen this life to learn, nurture, and understand the ways of this universe. When I elected to walk this place called Earth, I donned a suit of flesh. Through this suit, I perceive that which is around me through my five senses. It is the way of this world, the laws of this universe. In my heart however, I vaguely remember the other side, my true home, and I long to return.

My mind connects me to this world through my physical body. When I Journey, I leave my body and visit the spirit worlds. The faculties of my body do not function there. My mind connects to those worlds through other senses. Some call this the sixth sense, but it is more. In the spirit, I see not by my physical two eyes but my mind sees with a third eye. I see in a different dimensions than my two eyes perceived. I see all things as they were in the past, as they are now and how they will appear in the future. In the spirit, there is only the present. All that has past and all that is to come, is now, there is no time there as this physical world knows it.

Reflections

Years ago I learned that spirit beings have no age, sex, or any of the characteristic called human, yet we see them like ourselves, because the human form is a reflection of the spirit. When I was young this was hard for me to comprehend. One day as I sat by a quiet pond, I closed my eyes and looked at myself. Young, strong, full of life and virility, and then from my head a crown with three spikes appeared, each connected to one of the three spirit worlds. But when I opened my eyes and peered into the pond, the reflection I saw was not me. The tired eyes that looked back at me from that wrinkled face could not be me. The stooped frail body with hands twisted by arthritis was not what I remembered, and from where had come that gray hair? That is not me. I choose now to close my eyes when I gaze at my reflection.

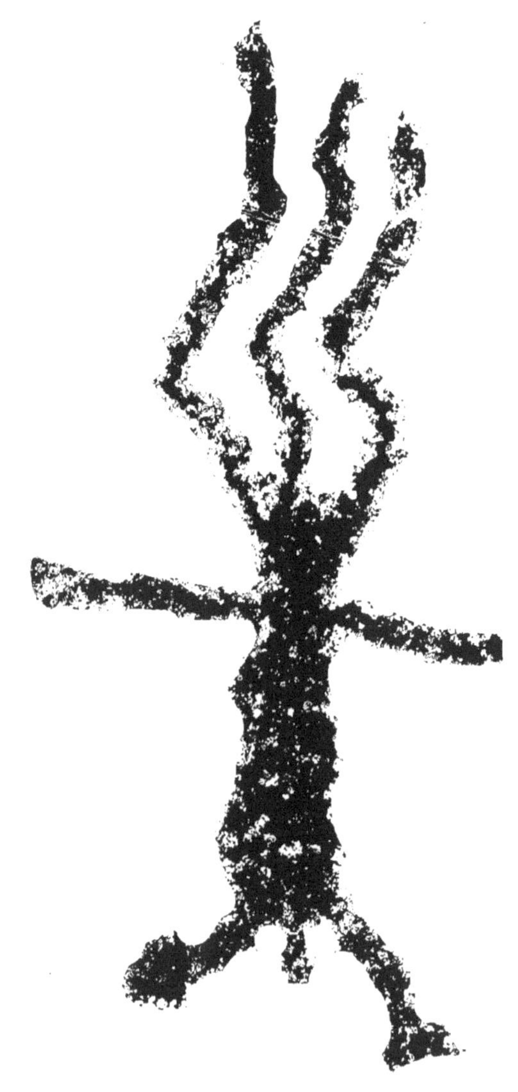

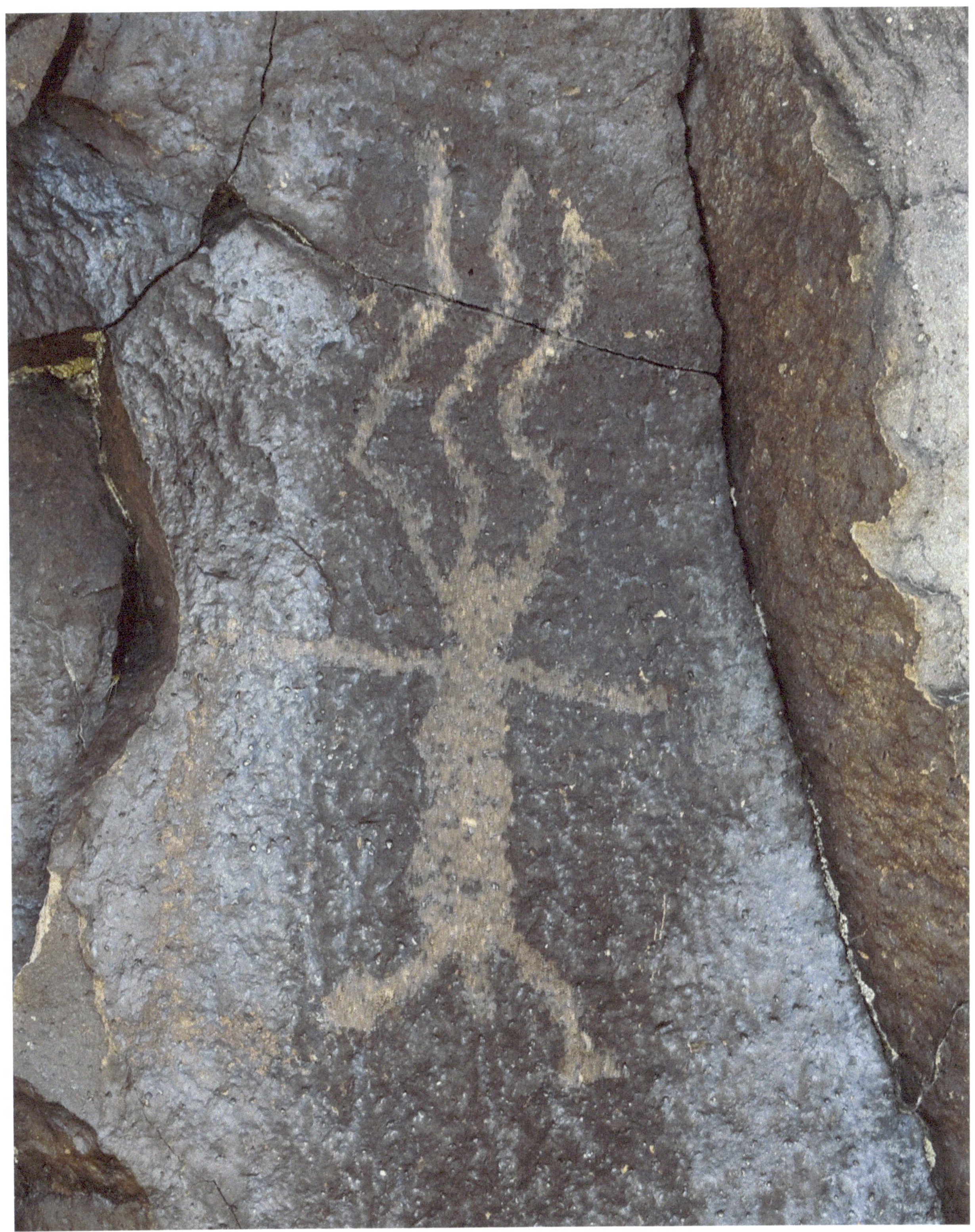

The human spirit that dwells in us is ageless, in our minds we see our spirit, with our eyes we see only our body.

The First Lesson

I come to the canyon with lofty ideas, without fears or worry. My head is full. I have said to myself that I will visit the lower world today to discuss my dream with the Wise Ones and show them how clever I am, and tell them that sit on the Wise Council, how wise I too have become. They will be proud of me and shower me with accolades.

What, the door to the lower world is closed? The keeper has locked it. I know he stands on the other side, so I knock. I pound and call, but no response. The echo of my voice mocks me, I turn away in despair.

Cold and alone, I walk the middle Earth. I have walked here many times before. Circles of many lifetimes tell me that my learning is less than complete; I have much more to learn. Each time I have completed a life cycle and discarded my Earth bound body; I journey to the great river in hopes to crossover once and for all. I stand by the water's edge and wait. Reflecting on what I should have done or could have done, and weep. I had come with so many good intentions, where have they all gone? Spent like a fool on self, now my pouch is empty.

Regrets, a trivial luxury I cannot afford. I am learning that kind words unsaid and good deeds undone are the sins that keep me bound. Kind words and good deeds are the simple acts that fill the heart with gold. Why is it that the simple things are so hard to learn? Can I think, tomorrow I will change my ways, will I have another chance to say, you have done a good job, you are fine looking or I love you? So when again I stand at the edge of great waters and search the reflection of my life how will I judge myself? Kindly I hope.

A man or woman must judge his or her own life. By reflecting on their Earth walk with frequency and choose to correct their path they will find peace, joy and happiness. Refusing to see their reflection before their time on Earth ends will cause them to suffer the shame of that which they left undone. Knowing the truth of their folly, they will pick up the mantle once again and repeat another life cycle, determine to do it right.

I will place my mark upon the canyon wall and declare I am a foolish man. Maybe someone will see my scratching and realize their stupidity before it is too late. My mark is on the wall beside the tree of life. The cycles of my life, like the growth rings of the tree, tell me, I am growing. I will walk from the canyon today with my eyes open. My Earth cycle is near complete and yet it is not too late. Maybe at the end of this life, I will judge myself worthy. I will have remembered to feed the poor, help the infirmed and lend a hand to my neighbors. I will remember to speak the words of encouragement and praise and tell all I see they are comely. I will not forget to say, I love you.

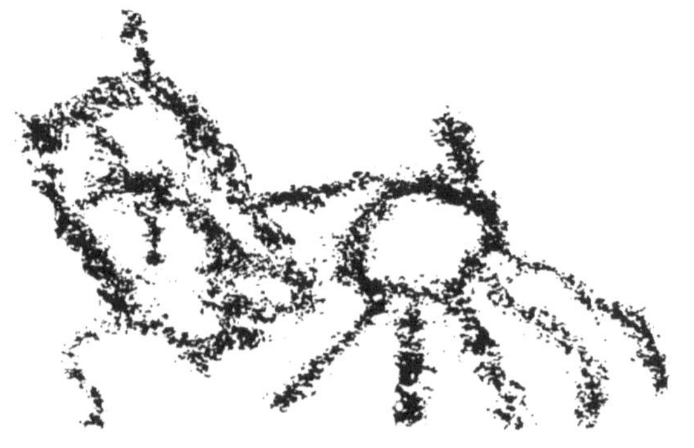

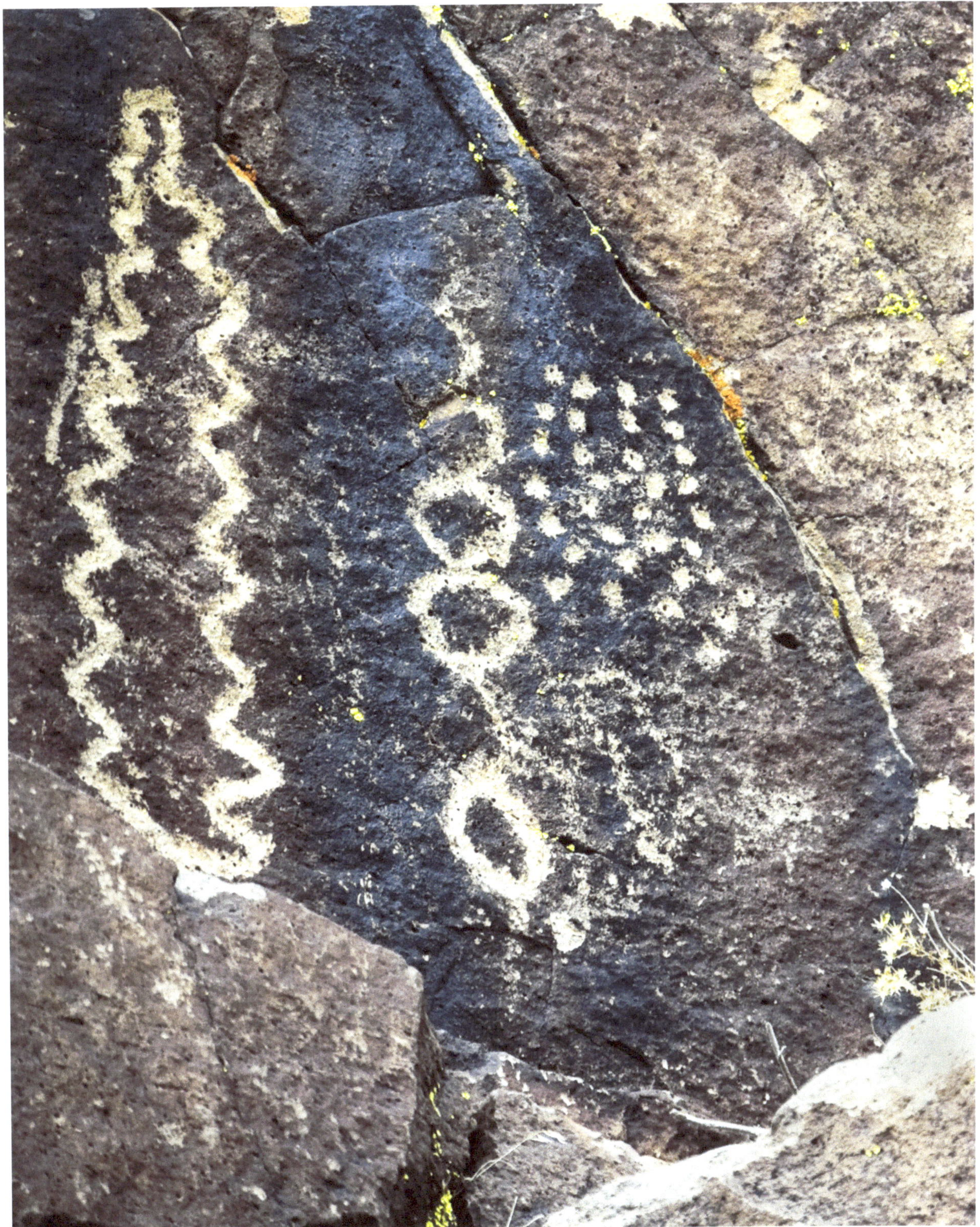

Simple images that represent thoughts and ideas were the beginning of writing, however some images transcend words and writing.

Animal Guide

I sit in my Lodge and tend the fire, as I stare into flames as figures dance all about me. As always, the flames mesmerize me. Slowly I close my eyes so I may see. Ravens chatter about the strange other people who walk the middle world with their eyes open but cannot see. After a time I begin to see the world that I cannot see when my eyes are open. With Owl on my right and Badger on my left, they accompany me as Bear guides us. Deep into the warmth and comfort I go, into the lower world I journey.

I know my animal guides are always here to protect me, comfort me and give me counsel, but today I seek a special friend. I learned of my animal guides from the stories of my people. Children's stories some call Fairytales and Myth. Animal guides are spirits in the shape and form of animals that assume and possess the power of that animal. They come and go and visit us at will. We see them out of the corner of our eyes or in the shadow sitting quietly beside a tree. They are always benevolent and we should never fear them. They wait in silence for our direction. Ever patient, ever vigilant, they are ever our protectors.

As I walk, I look about and see the beauty of the lower world. It is much like the middle world only there is no sun. The sky is light, but there are no clouds and there is a calm stillness in the air because the four winds do not blow here. In the lower world it is always spring, the flowers always bloom and there is abundance. There is no need for rain yet the streams always flow. In this place, sheep graze in the meadows while ravens, foxes and coyotes play together. Eagles soars the skies and lizards crawl on the stone. I know this place is where my journey really begins.

I have come this day for a special reason. I have come to see my friend. I can sense her presence but cannot see her yet. She sometimes likes to play the game of hide and seek but I know when I call she will always come. She never speaks with the words of the two-legged kind but she tells me much. At night, she guards my lodge, by day she guides my path, and though I may not always see, her presence I always feel. However, in this lower world, we can have a special time together. She is Lady Jaguar, and when at last I do see her, she shimmers, her spots glisten on her fine dark coat and her eyes glimmering gold. She is my most powerful animal guide. Today we sit beside the quiet stream, reminisce of good times past, and converse on the challenges of tomorrow. Today we choose to dwell in peace, joy and happiness.

At last I hear the sound that tells me, home I must return, and though I leave this place and Lady Jaguar, I know she is always with me. The fire has turned to ash and the sun is climbing high, I have returned to the ordinary, but no ordinary life I live with Lady Jaguar at my side.

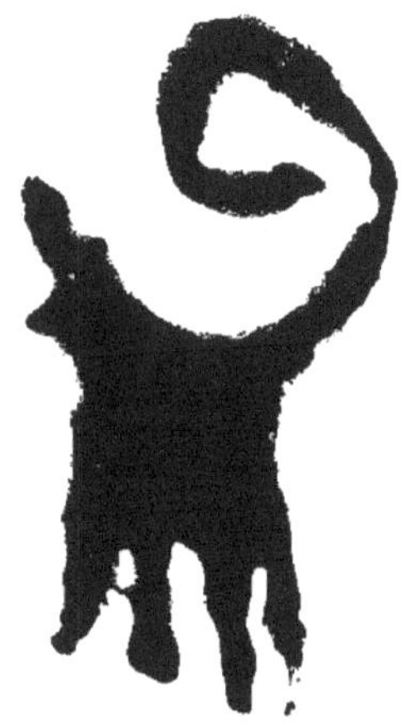

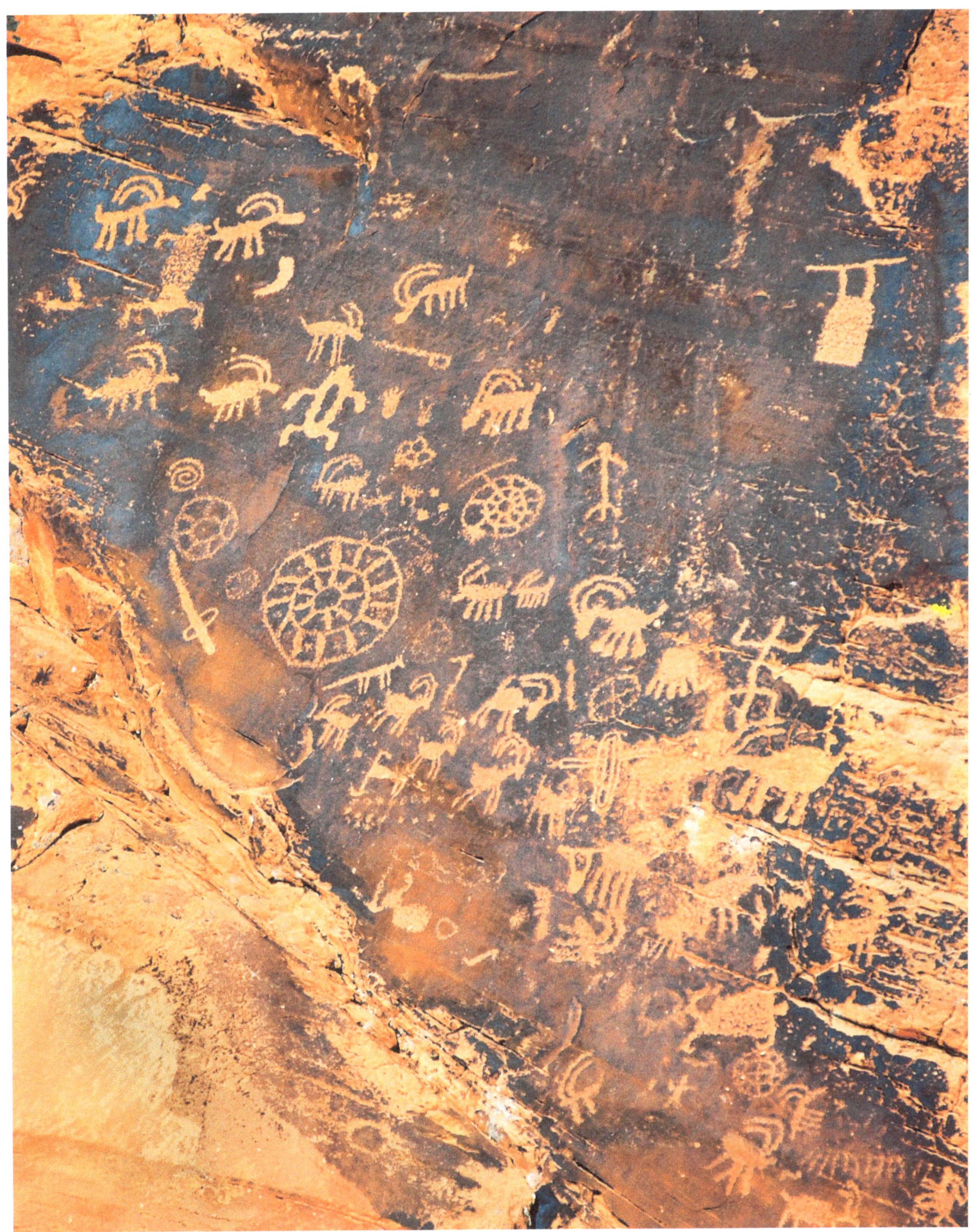

Countless images of animal guides have been pecked, scratch and draw on rock and canyon wall throughout the world.

The Call of the Shaman

All my life there was a yearning, emptiness, a feeling there was something more. I always knew it was there but didn't know what it was. The elders said it was The Call. "A call to what," I asked. "You will know when you find it," was their only answer.

I searched. I searched the city sidewalks and the country byway. I searched the books of wisdom and hallowed halls of schools and seminary. I asked of wise men, the fools, priests, clowns, monks and masters, but none could answer. They gave me their philosophy, but no answered. At last, I resolved to find a quiet place and go without substance or company until at last I knew this thing, The Call. There, lost between this world and the never world, I at last understood. I am a Shaman.

I went to the feet of the master/teacher and began to learn the way of the Shaman. I learned to heal the sick, make whole the broken heart and restore the soul. Then at last, I learned to Journey. Fully prepared, I was ready for my first Journey. The master/teacher taught me how to go within and find that special place. In trance, I found the entrance to the other worlds, but as I approached, I found it guarded by the gatekeeper who greeted me warmly, but would not let me pass. "Why can I not pass?" I asked the keeper. "The master/teacher has sent me this way."

"What are the three virtues?" He asked. "They are the keys you must have to pass this way?

I stood quietly for a moment and reviewed the master/teacher's words. He said, "Seek and you shall find, knock and it shall be open unto you."

"They are not the three virtues." He replied.

My heart sank as I tried to remember the master/teacher's words. I sought; I knocked, but found no answer, the master/teacher had not spoken of the three virtues. Discouraged, I was about to turn away when deep inside my mind words came, belief, motive and intent. They were not the words of the master/teacher; they were the words in my heart. No one can teach you the Way of the Shaman, it must come from within.

Belief

The first key is belief. One must believe with all their heart there is another realm, the realm of spirit and the supernatural. Beyond the veil of the physical world are other dimensions that cannot be experienced with our five senses.

Motive

Motive is key number two. An individual must be motivated from a pure heart. Greed, want, lust and desires of the flesh motivate the physical world. To enter the spirit world you must overcome your physical world. If your intentions are to manipulate the physical world by use of the spiritual, you will be in disharmony with the universe. You may gain an advantage for a short time but in the end you will destroy yourself.

Intent

One must declare their intent before they can pass. The realm of the spirit is not a place of amusement for those who are on an Earth journey. Humans are physical bodies inhabited by spirit beings. When we choose to incarnate for an Earth journey, we do so for a purpose. It is through the cycle of an Earth life that the spirit experiences and gain knowledge of the physical. When we journey to the spirit world, we do so to enhance our understanding and knowledge or to help others. When in the flesh, we must have a reason to journey to the spirit world. Without intent, the gateway is always blocked.

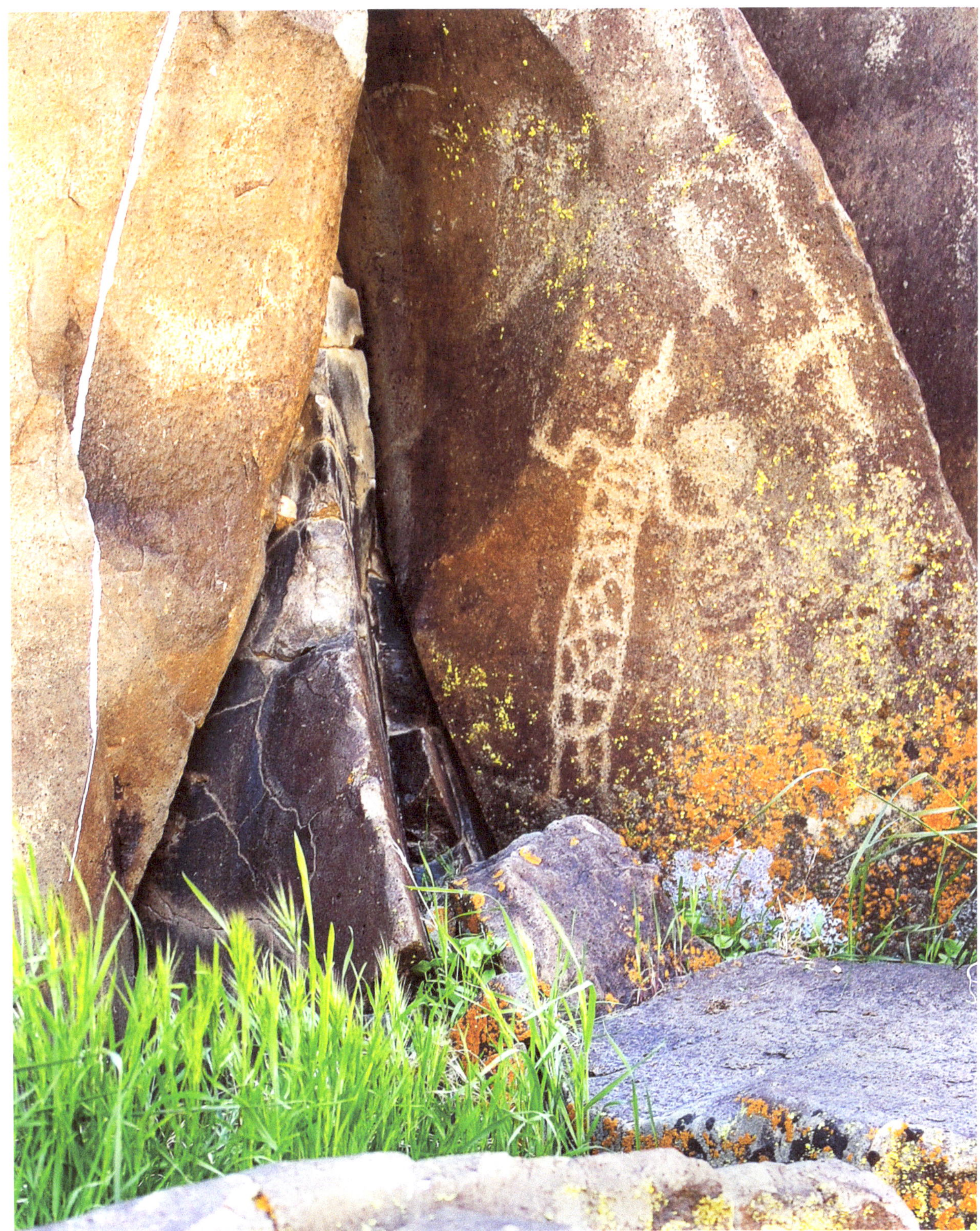

The gate keeper guards the portal to the other worlds, without the key you cannot pass.

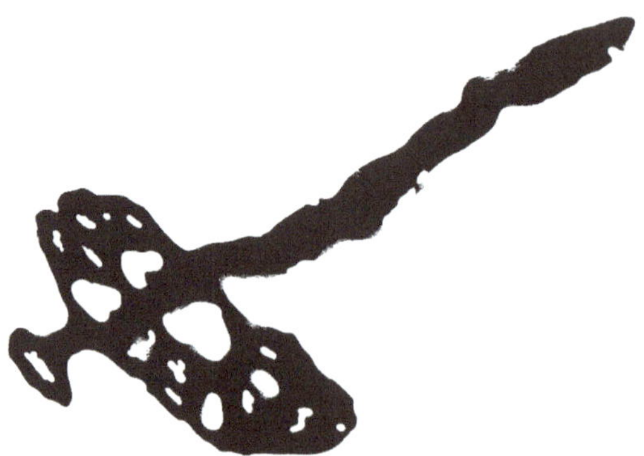

The Image of the Shaman

I have come a long way since I first felt the calling. Some may say it is a sickness or disease of the mind but I know now it is a call of the spirit. On the mountaintop, I realized that I must walk this way or die, so all I can do was try. In earnest, I have studied the ways of the ancient ones and learned the stories of my people. I have received the teaching of the world and the training of the wise. I have faced the foes of darkness and survived. Deep in the darken cave I learned the Way of the Shaman and now at last have become alive.

But who am I? There are so many things I am. How can I choose just one of me when inside me I am so many? As the poet sings, I've been a priest, a poet, a pawn and a king, an artist, a healer, a husband and more. At last I see, I am all these things and more. I am a Shaman. Whether the world chooses to believe or not, I know who I am.

I can assume many forms and can change at will. When someone tries to define or explain Shamanism, it is impossible. Snow is made of many snowflakes, and every snowflake is different, therefor all snow is different, it is better to enjoy the snow than try to understand it. So to, it is better to simple embrace the Shaman than try to understand the Shaman., Remember the Shaman you see today is not the Shaman you saw yesterday, nor the Shaman your will see tomorrow.

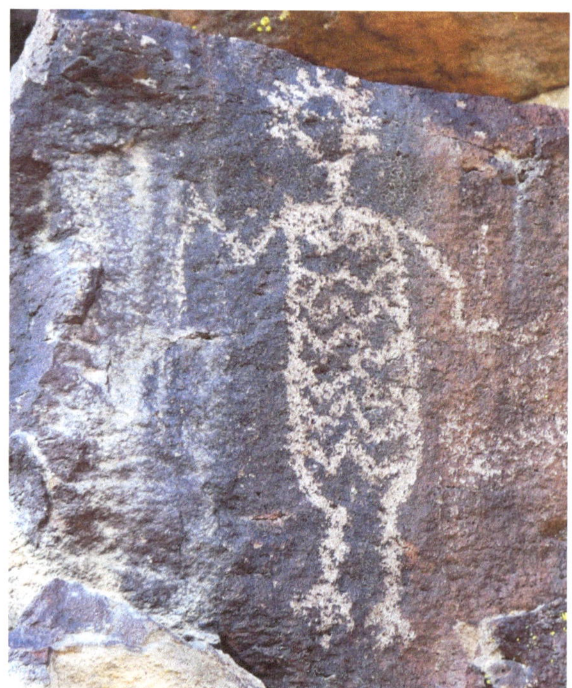

The Shaman see themselves with a headdresses reaching outward to the universe, with the feet of eagles signifying flight and the a medicine bundle in their hand.

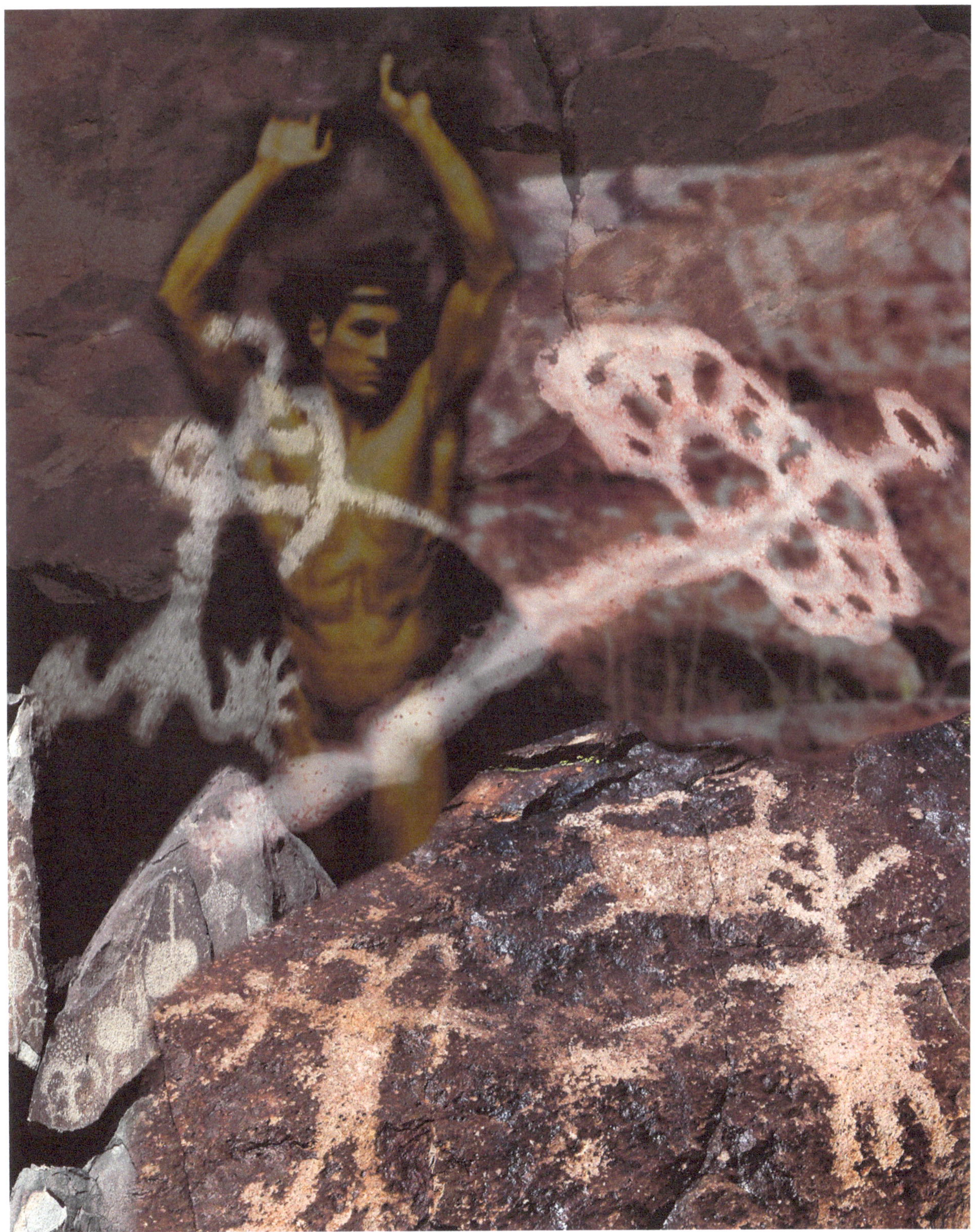

The Image of the Shaman Montage — Shaman see themselves as spiritual warrior, doing battle for their people.

The Cycle of Life

We are born dependent on our parent's substance and nurturing. Throughout childhood, we grow under their care and nurture until we at last become adults. We marry and may have children of our own, in time we grow old and die. This is the cycle of life.

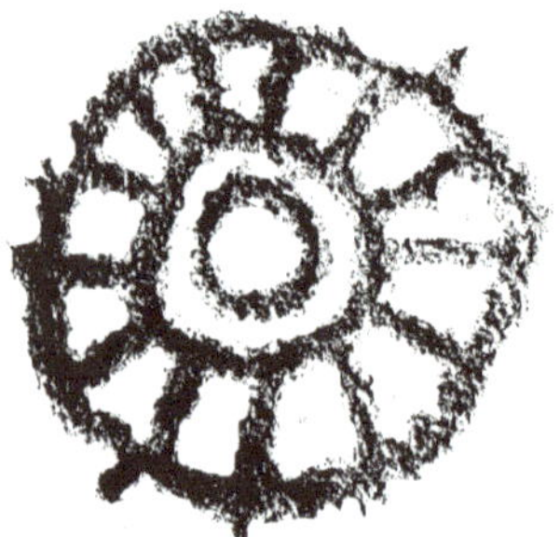

Beyond the Ordinary

Shamans have many extraordinary gifts and abilities and use their talents to help their people in various ways. They are storytelling teachers, sometimes called mythmakers. They teach the way of this Earth, how to live in harmony with nature through their stories and with them they make known the ways of the Great Mystery. They can see and journey beyond the ordinary to the spirit world through trance.

Shamans learn the art of making medicine and healing the sickness in body with herbs and treatments. With the use of soothing touch they can relieve pain and manipulate bones, and with herbal tonics, they can renew the infirm. Their gifts are awesome and sometimes feared.

Shamans comfort the dying, not just with words and deeds, but at times by their physical presents alone. Then the Shamans accompany departed souls to the other side where they can find rest. This ability makes them both admirable and intimidating .

The Shaman heals the sick and makes whole the soul by retrieving lost fragments. When a person is injured or suffers emotional trauma their soul fragments as a coping mechanism. When the trauma is over the fragmented soul should return, but occasionally a fragment does not, it gets lost. When this happens, the Shaman can find the lost fragment and return it. The Shaman achieves this by Journeying to other worlds in a ritual called Soul Retrieval. In a trance the Shaman searches for the person's fragmented soul. For the Shaman it may be as simple as finds a lost coin or it may require a fearsome battle with a spirit being, where the Shaman must fight the spirits of darkness in order to retrieve the lost fragment and return it.

The Shaman must sometime make themselves into terrifying other-beings to fight the foes of darkness. They become whatever form they can image; their human form does not bind Shamans. They can reinforce this other-being by making images of this form on the canyon wall so others may see them as they a appeared in the spirit world

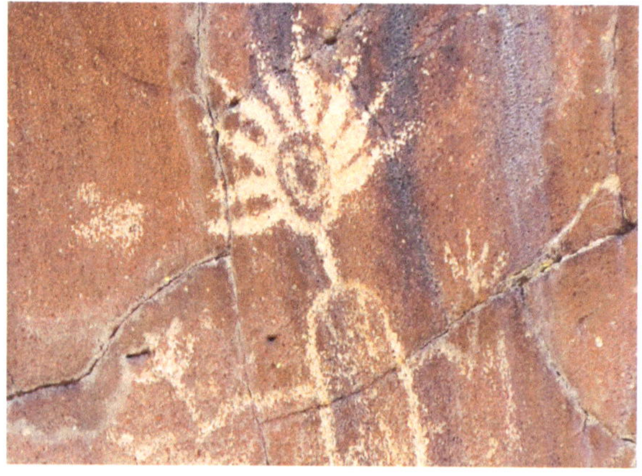

At times a Shaman must make their appearance awesome.

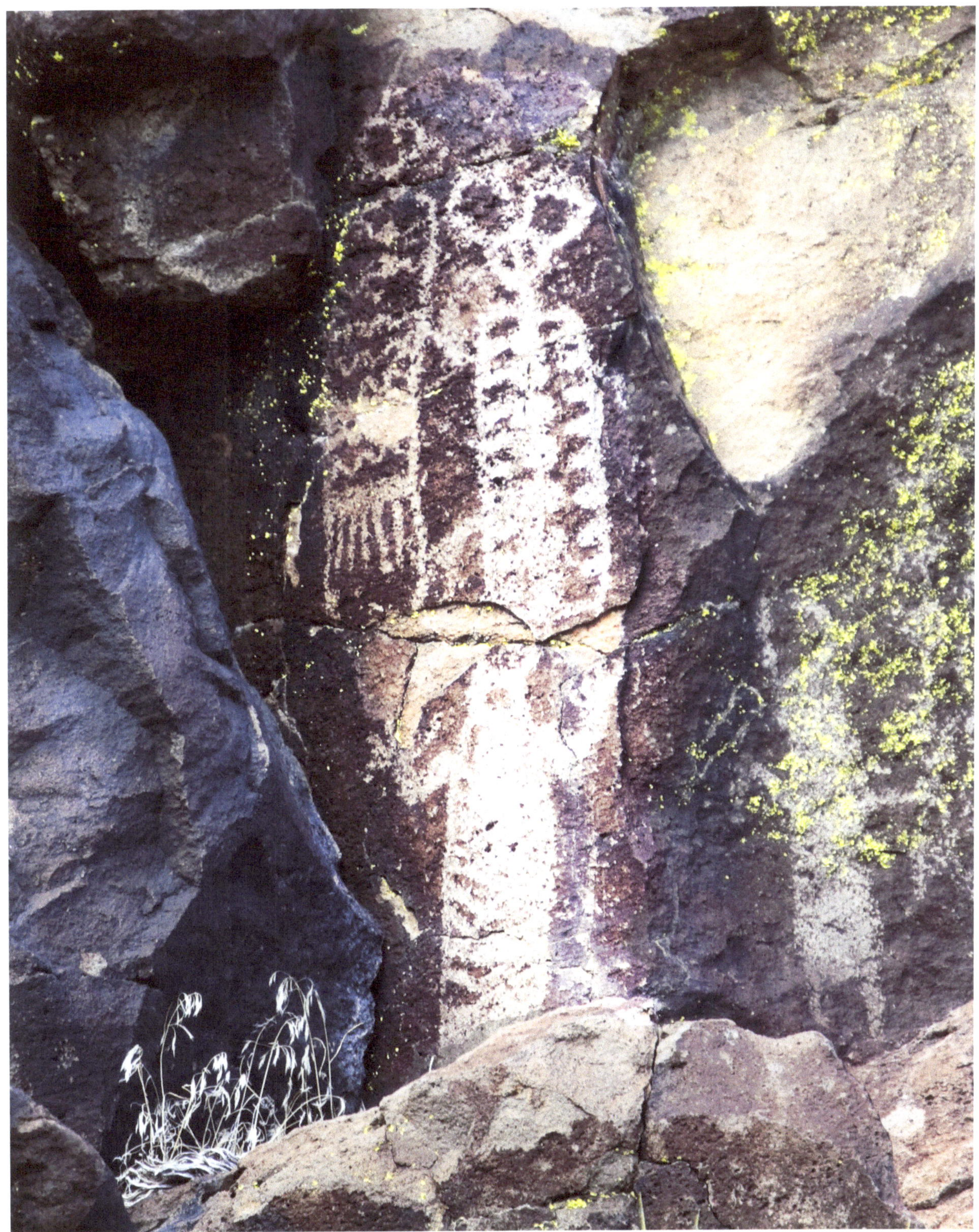

High on a cliff the Shaman looks down with its ominous stare from huge eyes that see all.

Into the Abstract

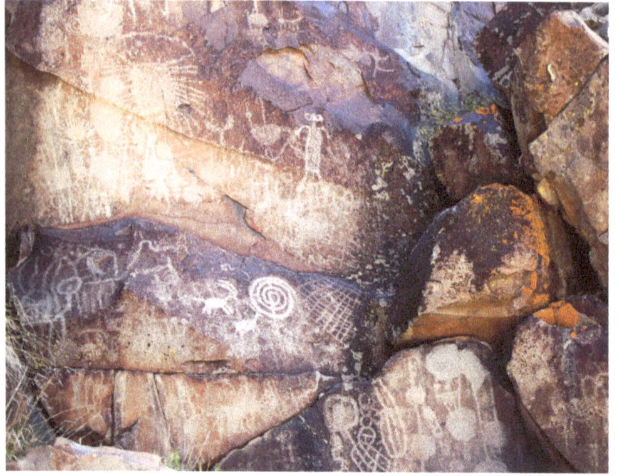

Details of panel shows a variety of images, some recognizable and some abstract. The symbolic language of the Shaman is not intended for the uninitiated.

I am shaman and I have eyes to see what others cannot.

Others look at stones and see only rocks but I can see the spirit within. It is not a single spirit but part of the spirit connection with all other stone's spirits. It is all part of the Great Spirit. I see that all are one in the Great Spirit. The Great Spirit is in everything.

The same dust, minute particles that makes the stone makes the man. The beauty of the stars is the same that is in a woman, as the child is a part of the parent.

What the eye sees is an allusion. Only allusion is real. What the eye sees is no more real than the spirit that the eye cannot see.

Do not despair little one, we in this life journey are not meant to understand. Even the Shaman only get a glimpse of the Great Mystery through wafts of smoke.

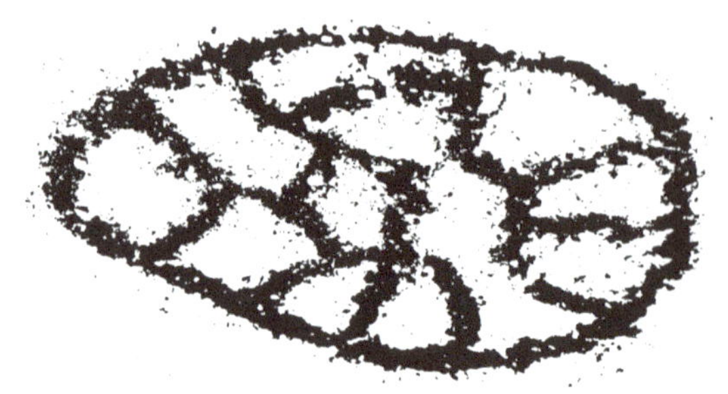

Logos

How can I draw what I see? In my head I see strange shapes. Some are meaningless but others represent thought and ideas. A circle with two dots and a line can be a face or a check mark can mean shoes. It makes no logic but it has meaning. Lines, dashes, circles, squares and odd shapes can mean nothing to some and can reveal to others the mysteries of the universe, even the very nature of the Great Spirit. Never dismiss the abstract as simple nonsense because you do not understand. Seek to understand the humble marks upon the wall; they might be the signature of God.

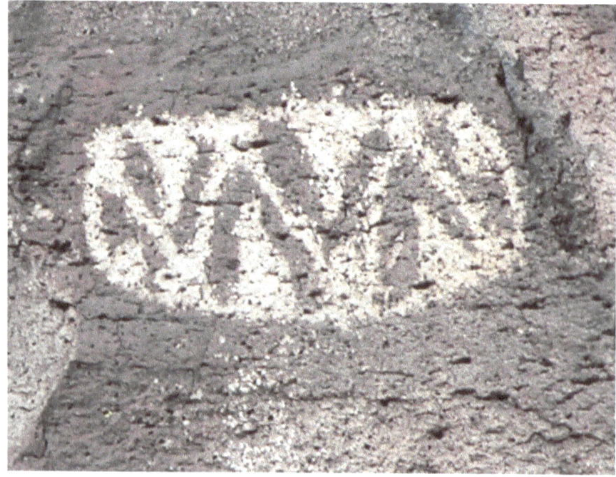

The zigzag patter is a common theme is Shaman art and has many meaning, but some are a form of signature.

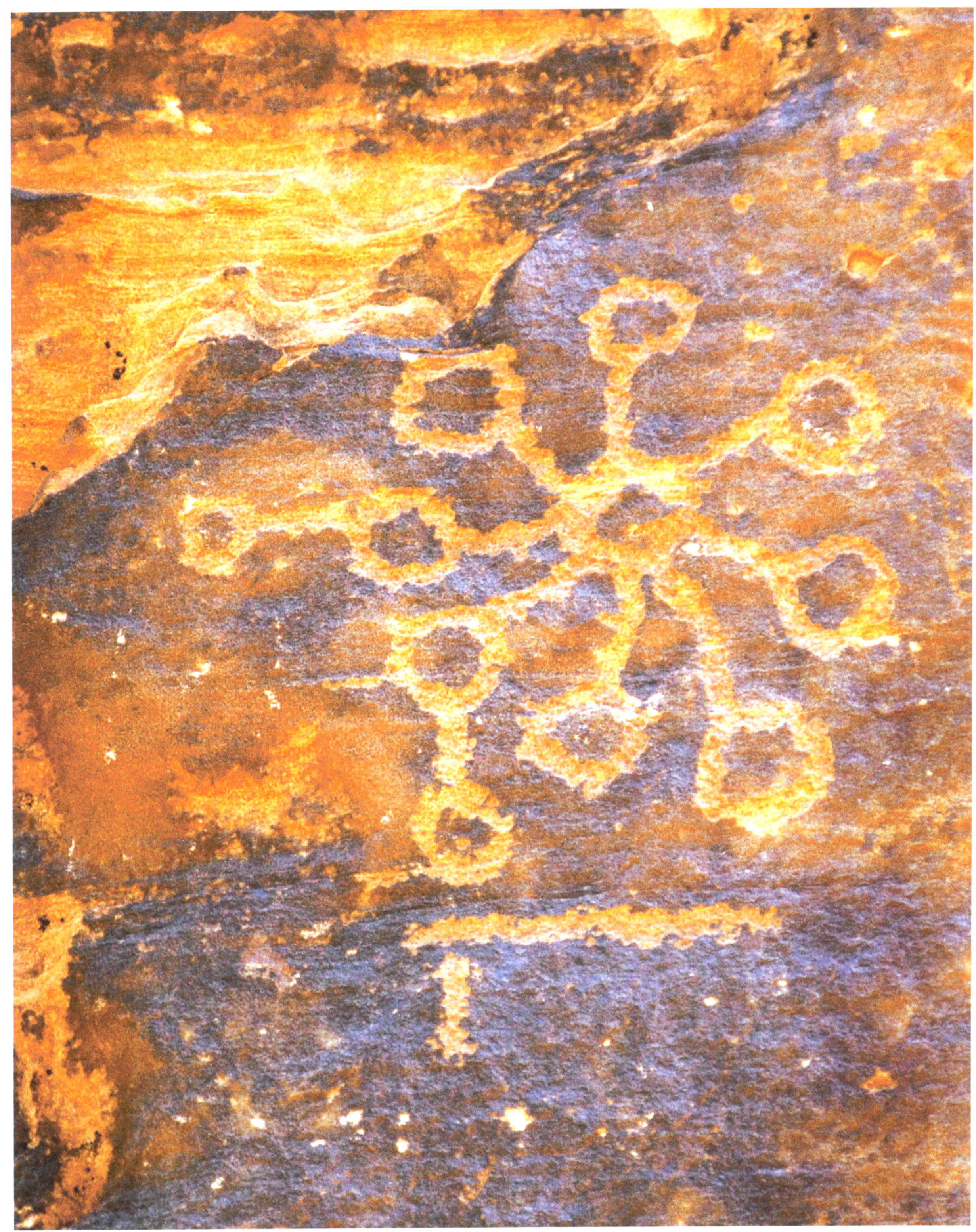

Drawing of the molecule, a microscopic life form or the mark or signature of a Shaman? The Shaman knows it is the latter.

Morning Comes

I lie awake, why? I don't know. The chill in the night, a strange noise or just the silence, whatever the cause I know sleep will not return. There are still several hours before the sunrises on another short winter day. Through the night the wind had turned the rain to snow and back to rain and now only the wind prevails, biting down from the southwest slope of the Tehachapi's.

With cold stiff fingers, I grasp the poker and spur the embers on the hearth to life. There are but a few small pieces of wood left beside the fireplace, so I rap and brace myself and step outside to bring in more. The firewood reserves are growing small, it is late February and I wonder if they will last until spring. With my arms full of precious fuel, I stand at the door captivated. The wind has pushed away the clouds and the silver light of a full moon glistens across the valley. My heart pounds at the sight of the remaining clouds that hang on the mountains to the north. The Spirit Clouds have returned, strange swirls of ghostly shapes stacked like pancakes in the moonlight. Some call them lenticular clouds; I know them for what they are.

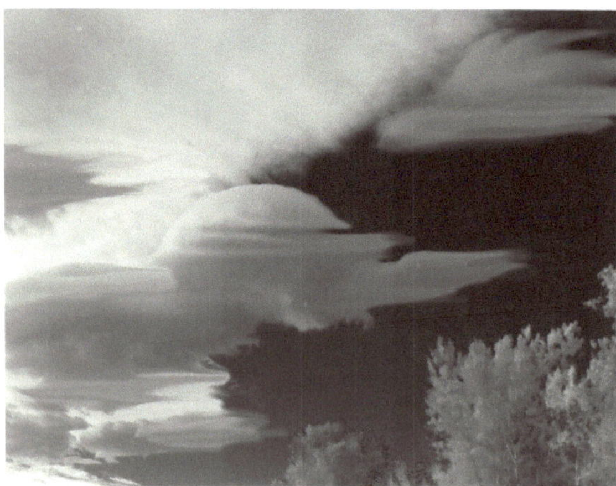

Infrared photograph of lenticular clouds

Absentmindedly I drop the wood beside the fireplace with a clatter. The noise startles me. I hope I haven't awakened my wife, she doesn't stir, only our three cats look at me annoyed, already disturbed by my invasion into their private time of morning. Sparingly I add a log to the fire and brew myself a pot of bitter barriers. With the warm cup in hand, I sit by the fire and ponder. The Spirit Clouds calls, how can I respond?

It's been many year since I first learned the way of the Shamans. Now my hair has turned to silver, the cold gnaws at my bone and the vivacity of youth has slowly stolen away. I can no longer journey across the desert to the sacred canyons high in the mountain to make medicine. Only in my spirit can I join the gathering of Shaman in the Sacred Canyon, to fast, pray, and seek the way of the Great Spirit. Only in my heart can I sit among the brethren and discus the mysteries. Only in my mind can I recall the meanings of the image carved on the Sacred Canyon's walls.

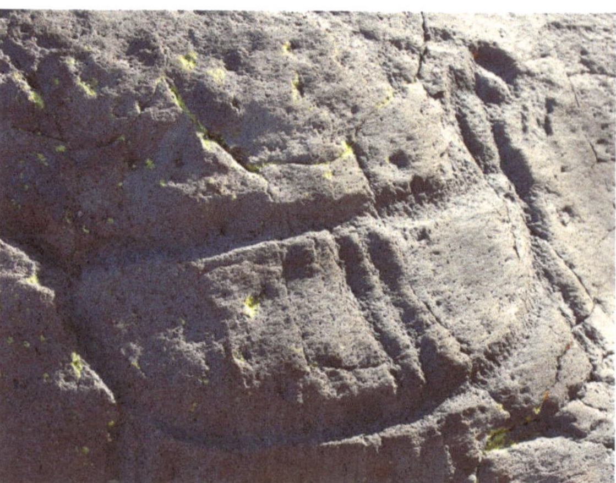

Images carved deep into some of the stones show repeated pecking, tracing the same image over and over. These are not mere practice carving, but a repeated action is not unlike praying a rosary or using prayer beads.

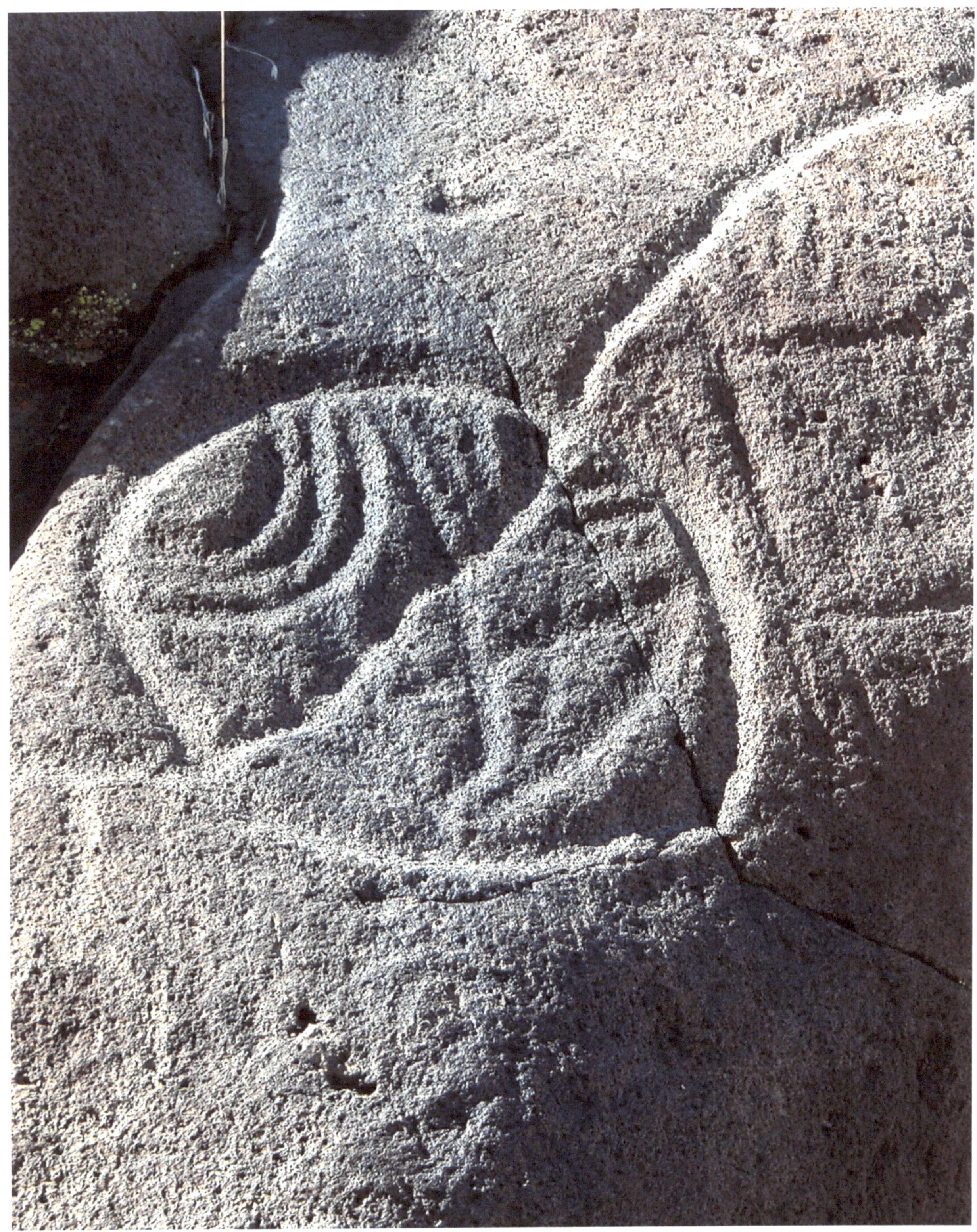

Abstract logo traced repeatedly in the hard stone until it was deeply etched.

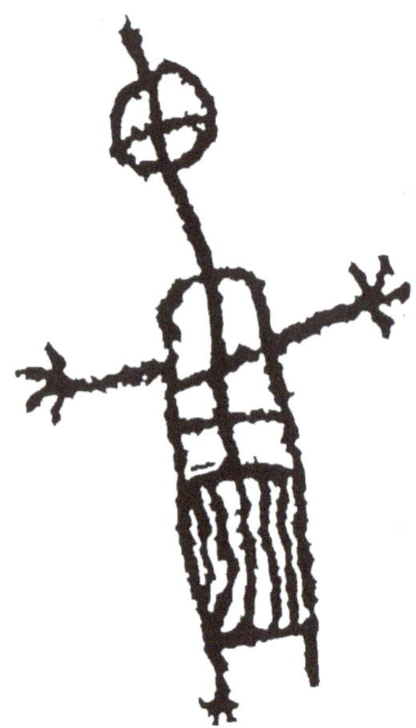

The Face of God

By the water I sit. My heart is sad, for all my life I sought the face of God, but found it not. Could it be that God has no face?

Then my spirit guide arose from the water and stood beside me and said, "Look around you, God's face is everywhere. Look at the face of the child in the cradle it is the face of God. The face of God is seen on your child, your mother and father and your friend, so too your enemy on the battle field has the face of God, even the face of the one that lies next to you in your bed radiates the face of God.

"God is every human that has ever lived. God is every animal, tree, plant, mountain, desert, rock and speck of sand. God is the storm and the shelter, the fire and the flesh, the laughter and the sorrow. God is the we and I of everything.

"God does not sit in a throne in the heavens doling out mercies and punishment upon the universe. God is the throne, the heavens, the Earth, the mercies and the punishment.

Jesus taught that the "Heavenly Father I are one. And this God in me is in you also." When you see yourself, your friends and family, your coworker and neighbor, your fellow human, friend or foe, you see God.

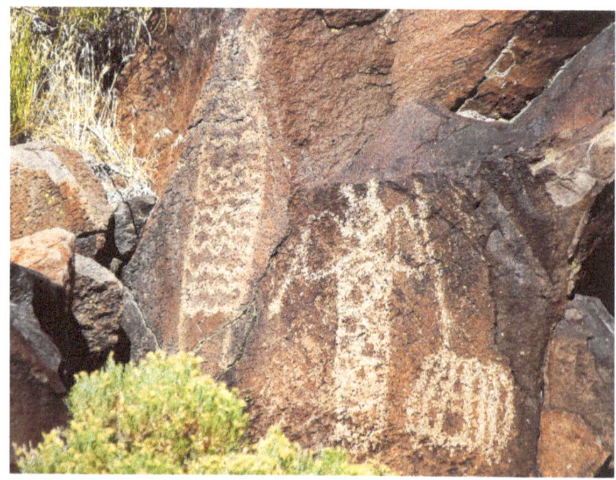

Recognize that God is in each of us is the beginning of transcendence.

"God and the entire universe are one. God is not good or evil. The universe is not good or evil. Everything is simply positive or negative. Everything that happens is good and bad, positive and negative. A cow is killed and we eat dinner. A home is flooded and a garden is watered. A storm destroys a city and a nation comes together and rebuilds it. Fire may destroy a home and yet out of the ashes new life begins. Cancer may take a child's life and the child's father is motivated to finds a cure that saves thousand, even the child of his enemy and then his enemy become his friend.

"Look in to the water, the face you see there is the face of God.

God is."

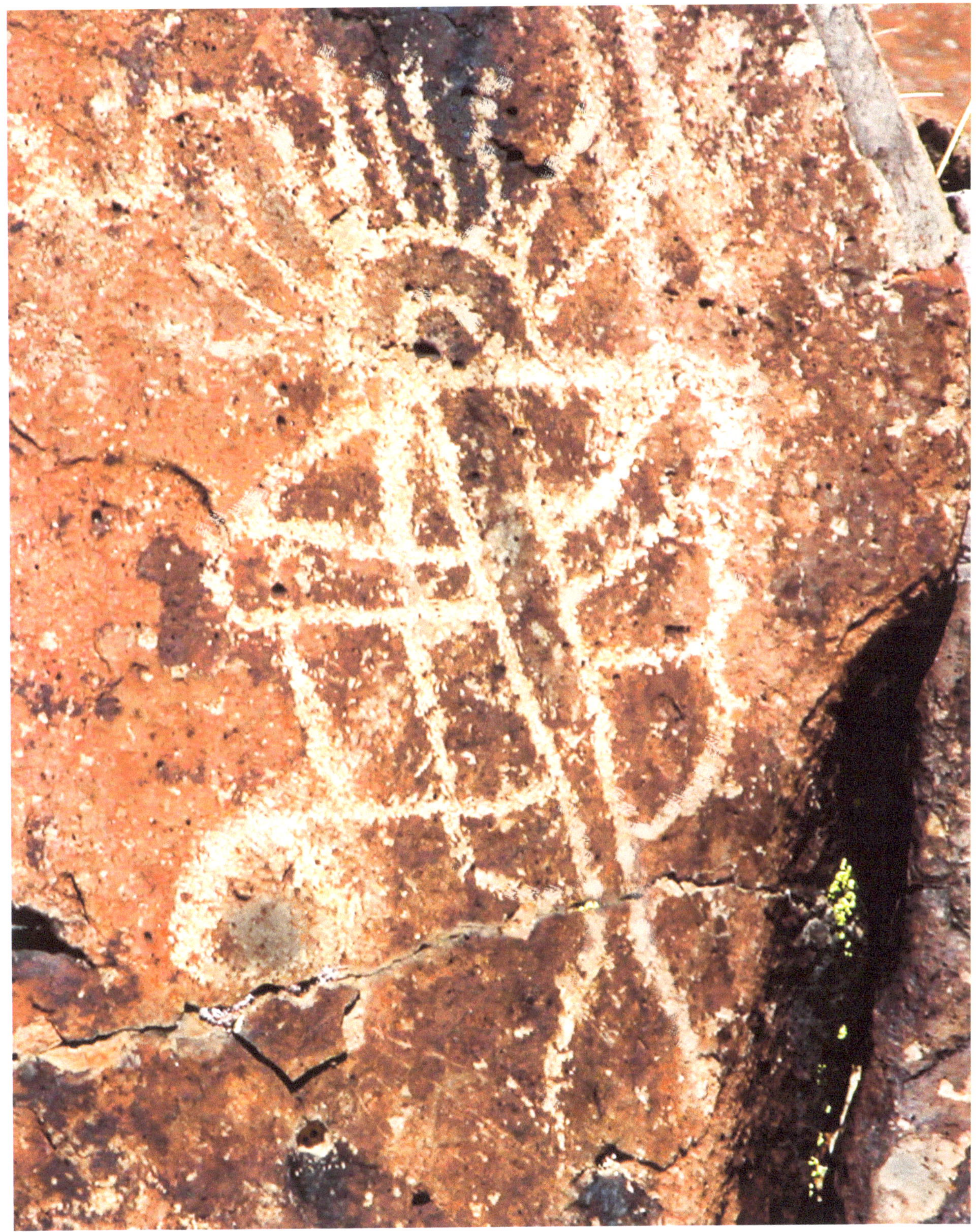

Throw off the cloak you hide under and reveal the God in you.

Good Medicine

Preparation for the Journey

Throughout history the Shaman has been the provider of Good Medicine, be it in the form of finding ample food and sweet water, provided knowledge of healing herbs or setting bones and dressing wounds. Most importantly, they administered spiritual healing. The total health and welfare of the tribe was in their hands. Their success meant the community prospered and lived in good health. The Shaman's failure meant hard times for the people and doom for the Shaman in exile from the clan or death. Recent finding in places like Stonehenge; have uncovered bones of Shamans that have been ritually executed in places where human sacrifice was not practiced, evidence that failure to deliver was not a pleasant option for the Shaman.

The mark of the Shaman was first that of physical healer. The proof of their spirituality was their ability to heal the sick.

And Jesus knowing their thoughts said, "Why are you thinking evil in your hearts? For which is easier, to say, 'Your sins are forgiven,' or to say, 'Rise, and walk'? "But in order that you may know that the Son of Man has authority on earth to forgive sins"—then He said to the paralytic— "Rise, take up your bed, and go home." And he rose, and went home. Matthew 9:4-7 New American Standard Bible

The Need

The winter was cold and long and the spring short, now summer has come and the grass withers, game is scarce and the trees bear little. I have come to the Sacred Canyon. For three days I have been without substance as I wait. I prepare my heart and mind to find good Medicine for my people. At last I feel the time has come. With closed eyes, a wakeful sleep over takes me, a new journey begins.

An eagle called. I looked up, the great bird circled above on the thermals. Its decent was slow, with each graceful loop he grew larger until he blotted out the sun. When at last he landed, I stood to greet him. He looked down on me and asked, "Why have you summoned me?"

"My people need. The creeks are near dry and the plants and trees wither. The sheep have disappeared into the high mountains and the people are hungry. Many too are sick; their bellies are hot with the flux from bad water and little nourishment. If I do not find them food and sweet water soon they will parish. You must help."

The great eagle paced back and forth before me, his eyes searched my very soul. I could hide nothing from his penetrating gaze. Will he find my heart pure? I wondered.

He ruffled his feathers with a frill, turned and stood beside a large rock. "Get on my back." He commanded.

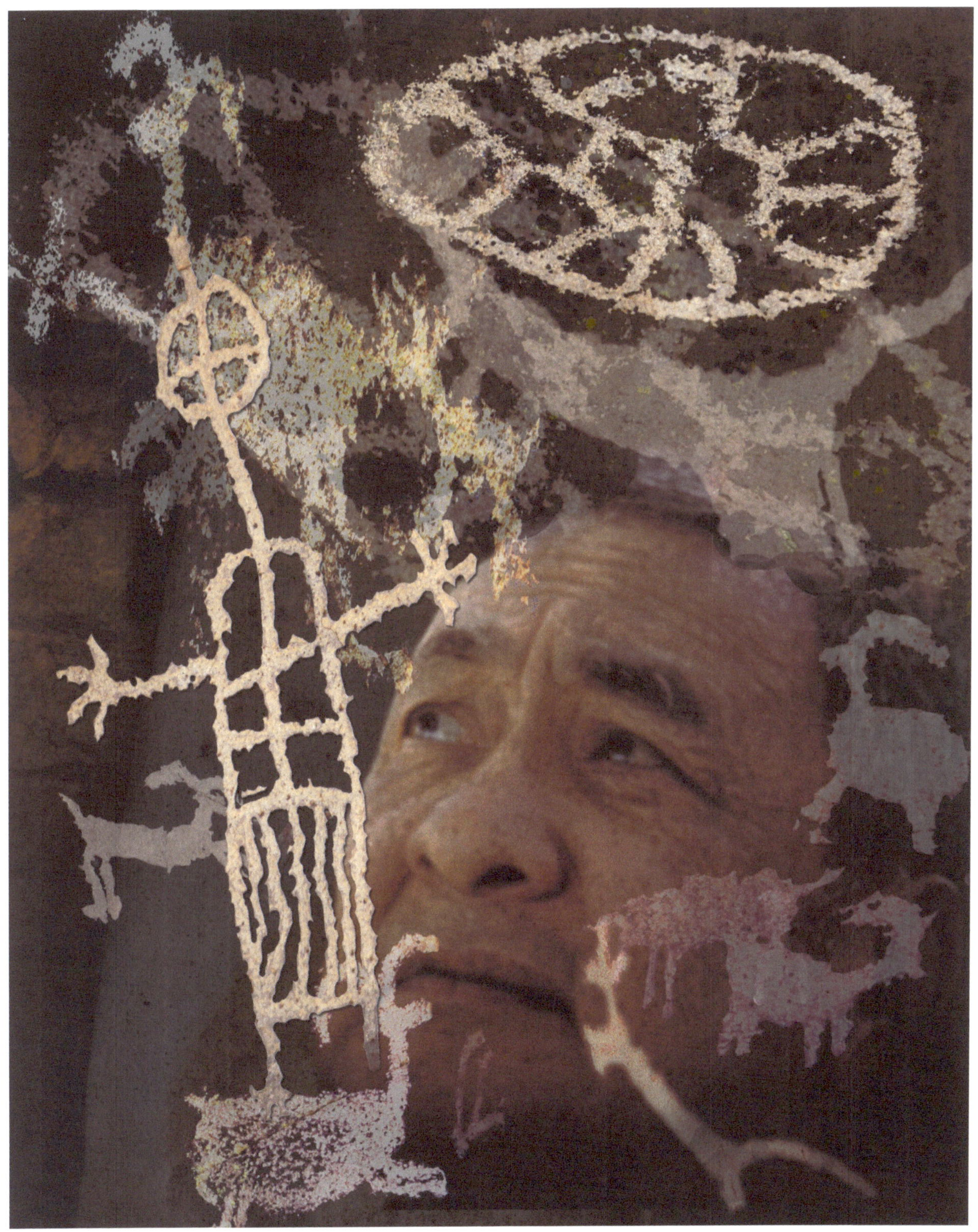

Good Medicine Montage —The Shaman depends on the spirit realm to meet the physical and spiritual needs of their people.

The Hunt

I climbed upon the great bird and grasped the feathers of his ruff. With a bound and a beat of his wings we were airborne. We soared high into the sky, below the canyon fell away. To the east was the great desert where no man lived and to the west, the home of my people. The eagle flew north, toward the White Mountains, and then descended. He circled low over a valley that I did not know. There was an abundance of pinion trees with cones ripe with nuts. In the middle of the valley was a lake and from it a stream flowed to the west. We followed the stream until I recognize were we were. "Thank you," I told the eagle. I knew now where to lead my people for pinion nuts.

The eagle screeched a joyful call and beat his wings. We flew up a familiar canyon, a dry canyon considered bad hunting grounds, but we flew past the dry falls, beyond where I had never traveled before. From this vantage point I could see herds of bighorn sheep, deer and antelope, and I knew I could direct my people to good hunting. The eagle beat his wind, banked and returned to sacred canyon.

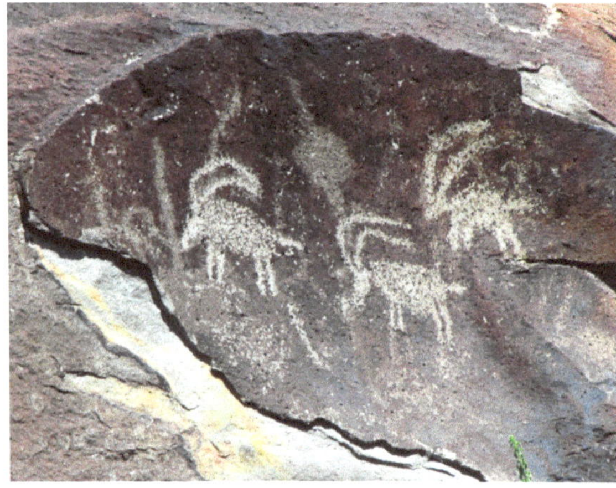

The Shaman pecked on stone what they saw in the spirit world, then by meditating on the image they could return to that place in spirit world.

I was once again seated by the canyon wall and the eagle stood before me. In a burst of radiant light he transformed into and handsome brave. He pointed to the canyon wall and instructed, "Draw what you saw."

I started to peck images of sheep into the dark desert varnish of the stone. My arm was tired as I completed the third sheep. "That's enough. Now stand back and look and the drawing. Look hard."

I stood and looked. All I could see were three sheep etched in the stone. "What am I supposed to see?"

"Touch the drawing. Trace it with your fingers."

I did as I was commanded. Nothing happened. I looked at the young man.

"Do it again. Keep doing it. You will see."

I ran my fingertips over the drawing repeatedly, but nothing happened. Then I began to-preserve images in the stone. Ripples, wisps and color changed, subtle at first, they began to intensify until they became swirling vista. I saw the canyon were we saw the sheep, and then other canyon filled with sheep and other game. The more I ran my finger over the images of the sheep, the more good hunting locations were revealed.

"These images of sheep are your hunter magic." The eagle man said. "Honor the image of the sheep and your people will not go hungry."

Without warning a bolt of lightning came out of the sky and struck the drawing of sheep near the tip of my finger, the force knocked me to the ground. I looked up at the sky and everything turned black.

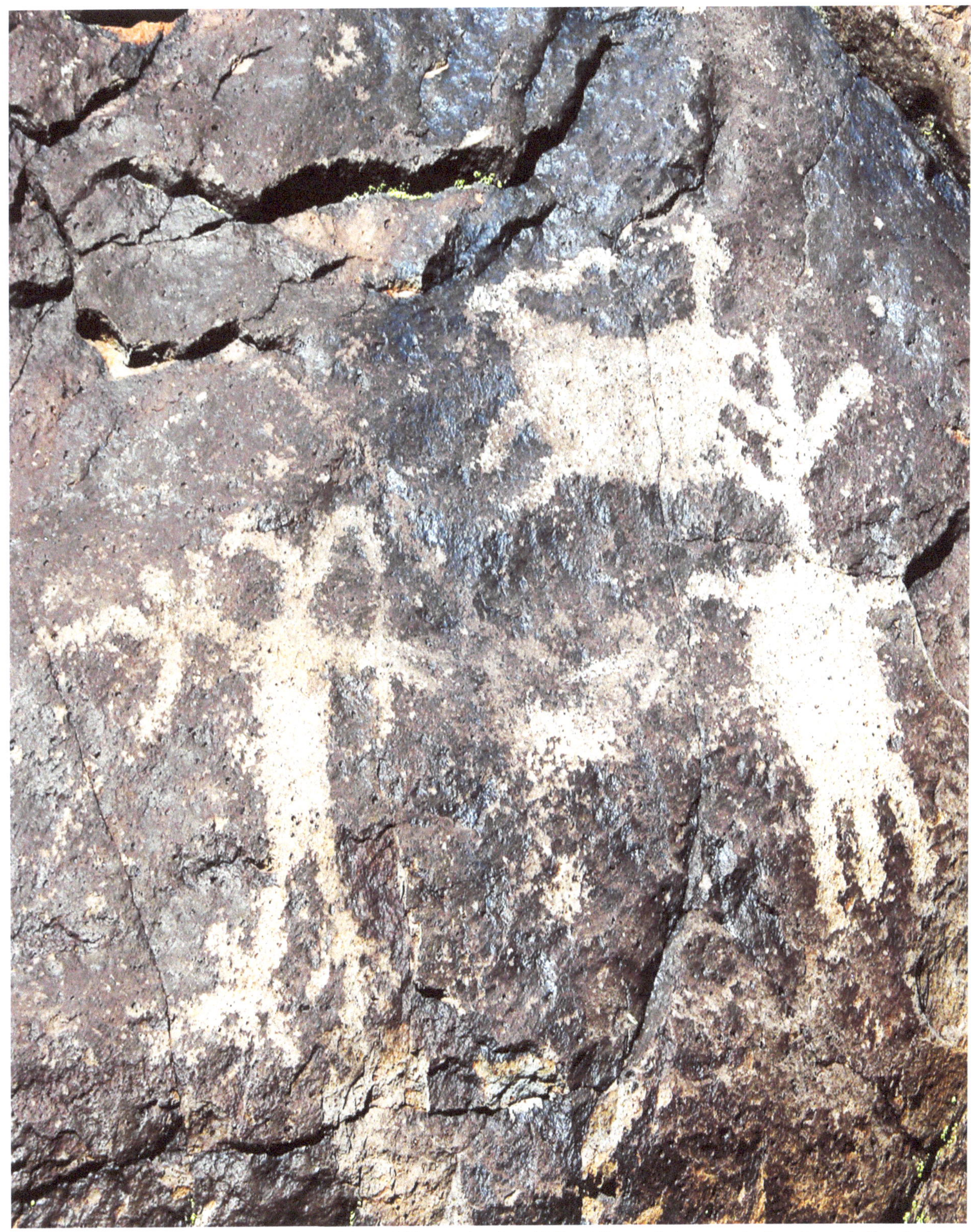

The Shaman, through journeying in the spirit, could learn of and could direct the people to game, fresh water and other food.

Healing to the Flesh

I awoke to the crackle of a fire, the eagle-man sat beside it. He had prepared a meal rabbit, pinion mush and a broth of herb. "Take, eat, and refresh yourself."

"Who are you?" I asked. He was not known to me. His face was strong and his eyes were clear and bright. On his forehead was painted the spiral of the spirit wind. His chests bore the symbols of lightning and on his belly were the lines of falling rain and the apron he wore was fringed. A cap of woven grass and quail feathers sat high on his head and when he stood, he was very tall, but his feet were those of an eagle.

I took the food he offered and it was good. I ate my fill as he watched. "You have a hearty appetite." He said, as we sat beside the fire.

"You haven't answered me, who are you?"

"You."

"You can't be me. You don't look like me and how can I be here talking to you if you are me?

"I am the image of your spirit, the part of you that soars from you when you journey. I am your eyes that see beyond the horizon, I am your wings that fly above the mountain, I am your arms that swim beneath the water, I am your knowledge that comes from the wisdom of ages, and I am your source. I am you."

I tried to comprehend his words, what was he saying? He was my spirit. That part of me the that left my body when I journeyed. Up until then I was taught to believe, a human was a body that had a mind that was somehow joined by a spirit, three separate facet of the whole human being.

"Your spirit, body and mind are one." The eagle-man continued. "The mind is where your thoughts dwell. The mind is not the brain; the brain is a part of the body. The mind is the whole of the human being and can collect information from both the body and the spirit, which it can receive or reject. You do not need to seek spiritual information any differently than carnal, it is constantly available, and all you have to do is allow your mind to accept it. You do not have to beseech God to see a bird, hear the babbling of a brook, smell a flower, taste the sweetness of honey or feel the gentle touch of your lover. Likewise, the things of the spirit are not mysteries hidden away, but are as close at hand as that which you know by your five senses. Good medicine, the ability to provide both physical and spirit healing are in your hand.

I turned to eagle-man and asked. "Why then must I separate myself from others, fast, pray, sacrifice and beseech God to know the things of the spirit?"

"Why? You tell me why you choose to make that which is natural and assessable so difficult. You have been taught that to be carnal and spiritual at the same time is not possible, yet you cannot help but be both, that is who you are."

The hot wind of the dessert swirled in my brain, my head ached and my thoughts were so rattled I could no longer think clearly. I told myself I was going insane and tried to clear these new words from my mind, but I could not. Somewhere deep inside me was that spark that witnessed I had heard a truth. In that moment I knew I could accept or reject it, but not change it, and if I accepted and walked in the light of that truth, I would forever be changed.

I reclined in the warm sand and let sleep comfort me. When I woke the next morning I felt a great comfort. The fire had died and my four-legged friends of the canyon had finished the remains of my supper. On the wall high above me, I saw the image of my spirit among a consul of spirits and smiled.

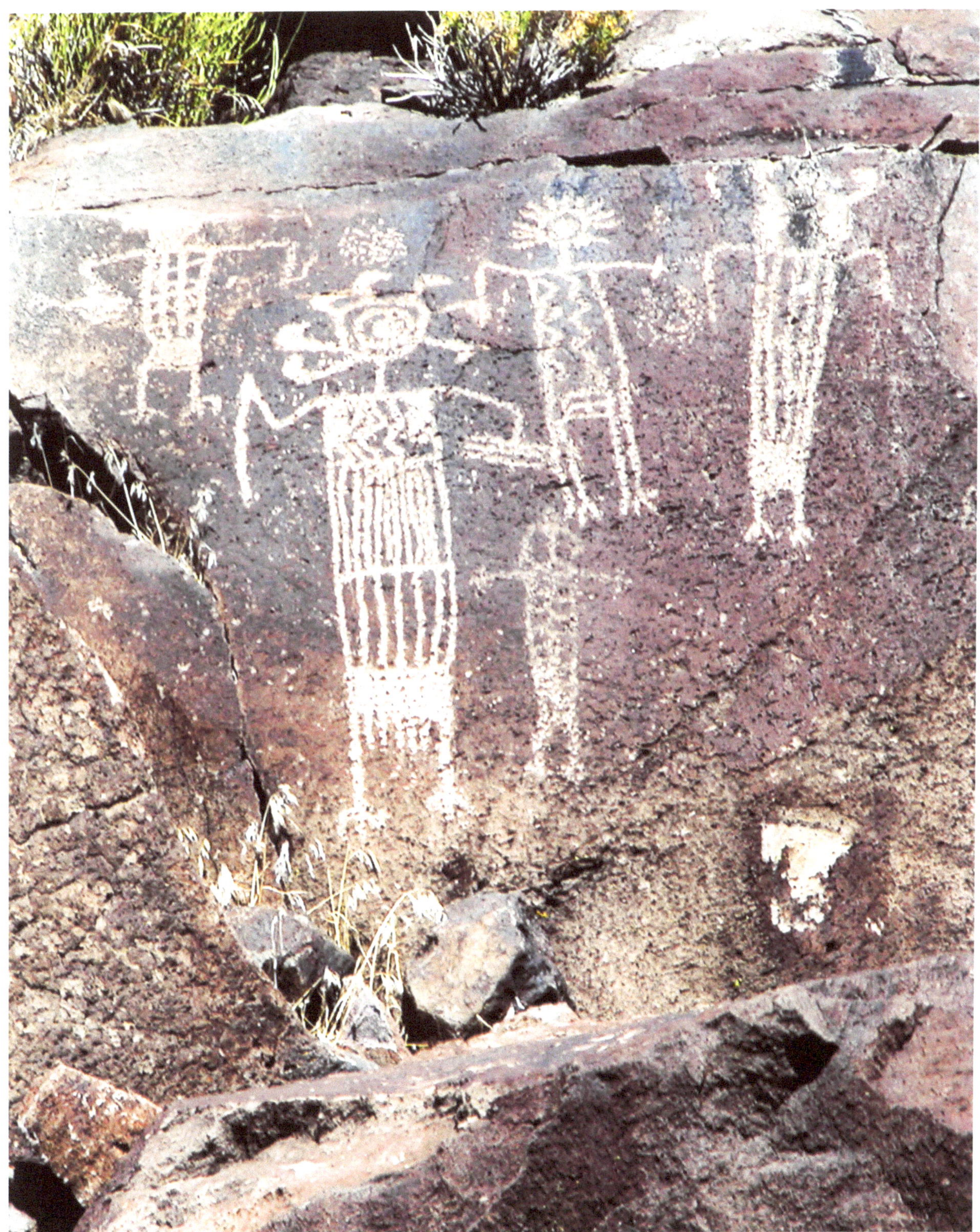

Images pecked in the dark varnish high on the canyon wall, the spirit being images of Shaman.

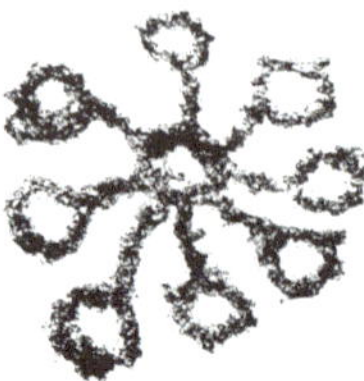

Spiritual Balance

The day turned warm so I sat in the shade to contemplate that which I learned the night before. There was joy in my heart and I was content to just sit, knowing I was exactly where I belonged.

We are all one in the universe, part of the essence we call God. This state of being is called spirit or spirit being, each is a part of the cosmos that is the consciousness of God. If we use the human body as a model of God, each of us is like a single cell. Skin cell, nerve cell, blood sell and so on, each individual and yet an inseparable part of the whole. Science is beginning to believe that the thought process is not just in the brain, but the human mind is throughout the entire body. The whole of this universe is the organism God and each spirit is like a single cell of God.

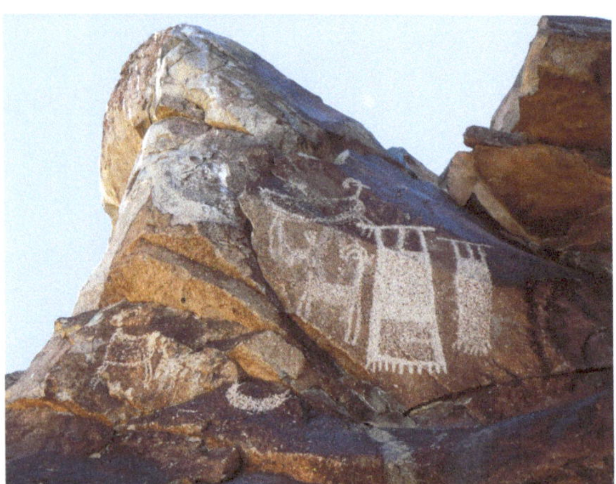

High above the canyon floor countless Shaman have made their mark, leaving their images to be shared by Shamans to come.

We come into this world to live in humanly flesh not by chance or accident, but through conscious choice to live and experience life on Earth. There is however a longing in all of us to return to the state of spirit. That longing for some is so great that they forget their purpose. They make up religious rules and piety laws trying bring themselves closer to God, when in truth, they and God are already one, they cannot get closer. This desire to be back in the state of spirit, prevents them from fully experiencing and appreciating their life on Earth.

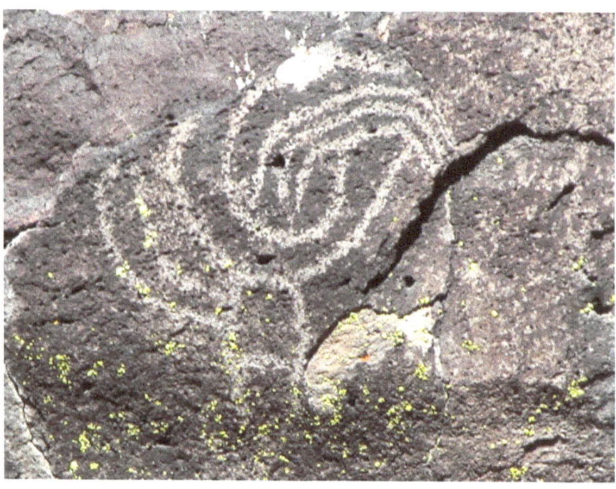

The Yen and the Yang, balance of life between the spirit and the physical is a delicate dance.

A balanced life is a life that recognizes we are but visitors here on this Earth and that while we are here we are to live life fully. In this life we need only to resist doing harm to others, walk in the light of our own way, knowing each has a different path to follow and to our own self be true. Judge not, condemn not and as much a humanly possible, love our fellow human being and all the creatures great and small. Walk softly, treat Mother Earth with respect and live and celebrate life.

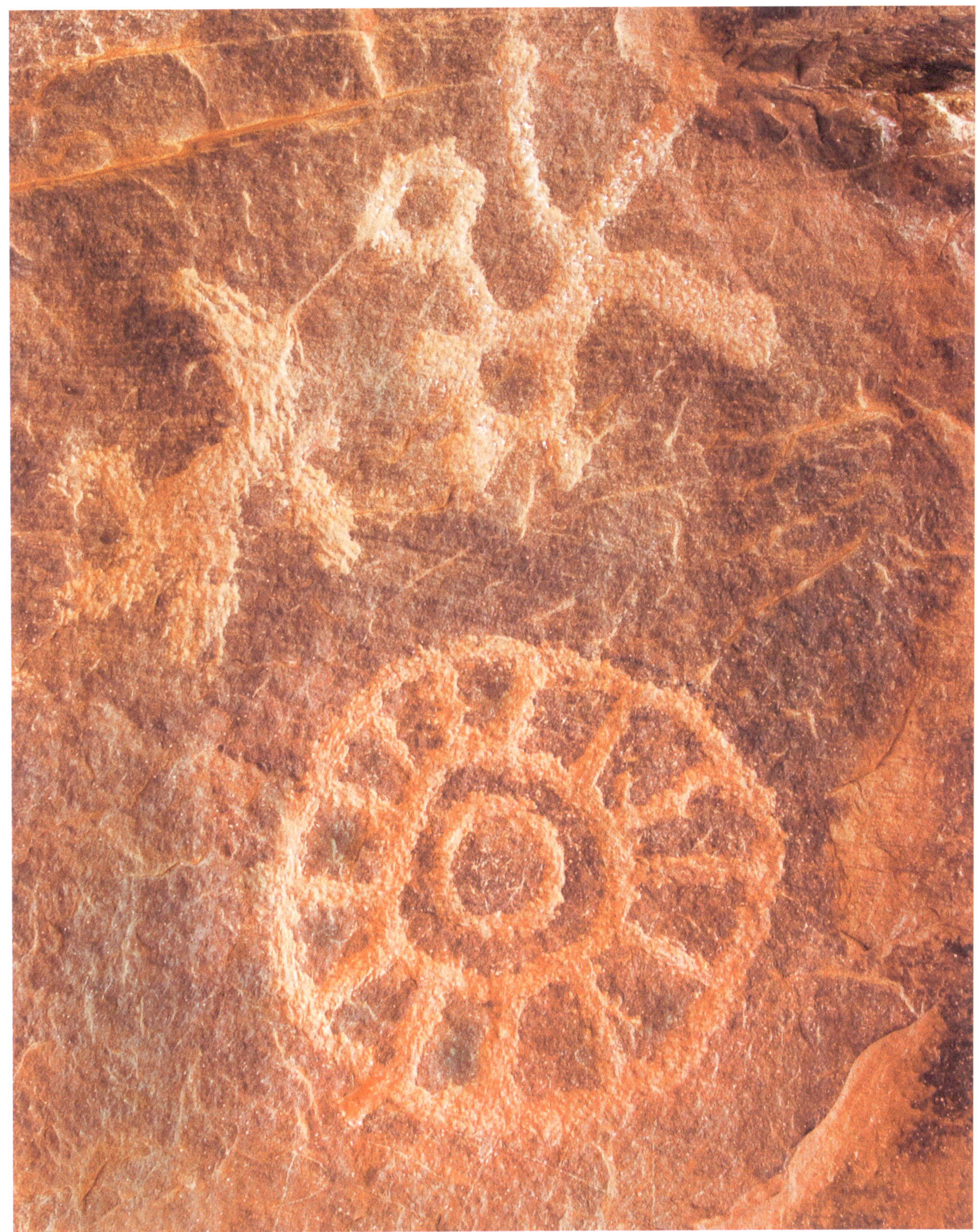

To balance our lives between the spiritual and the physical is difficult and we are easily distracted.

The Struggle

Why at times does life seem like such a struggle? Can it be we choose to make it so? It is said by some that life is a dance between good fortune and bad while others say good fortune is of our own doing. The consensus is that good and bad is judged by ones perspective. William Shakespeare wrote in *Hamlet,* "There is nothing either good or bad, but thinking makes it so."

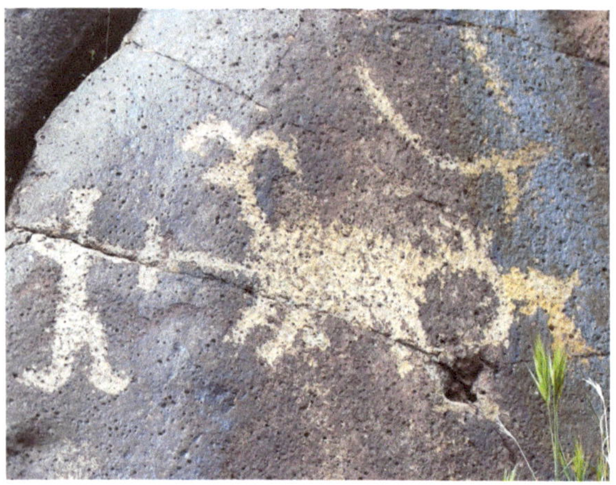

For there to be life there must be death. Humankind must kill and eat to survive, be it animal or plant.

In the universe what we perceive as good and evil is simply positive and negative. For there to be life there must be death. In our world we call it, the survival of the fittest or the law of the jungle, but in truth this is the law of the universe. Life is a struggle of balance.

For life to exist there must be death. This is not evil.

The Journey of Struggle

I find a quiet place beneath the shade of an aged oak tree near a tired stream and prepaid myself to ascend to the upper world seeking understanding. I wait in the stillness.

"Get up," the voice commands. "Get up and dance. When you turn to the right, is that good? No. When you counter to the left, is that evil? Of course not, yet some would say it is. The process of life is to struggle and this struggle is made of good and evil by your perception. There is no good or evil in the universe."

"Why, if there is no good or evil in the universe," I asked, "is there so much evil here on Earth? Surly you cannot say murder, rape and war is not evil."

"Come walk with me and I will show you the nature and root of evil."

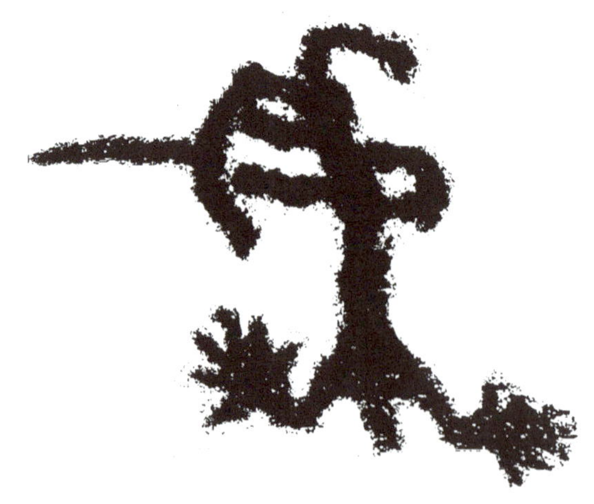

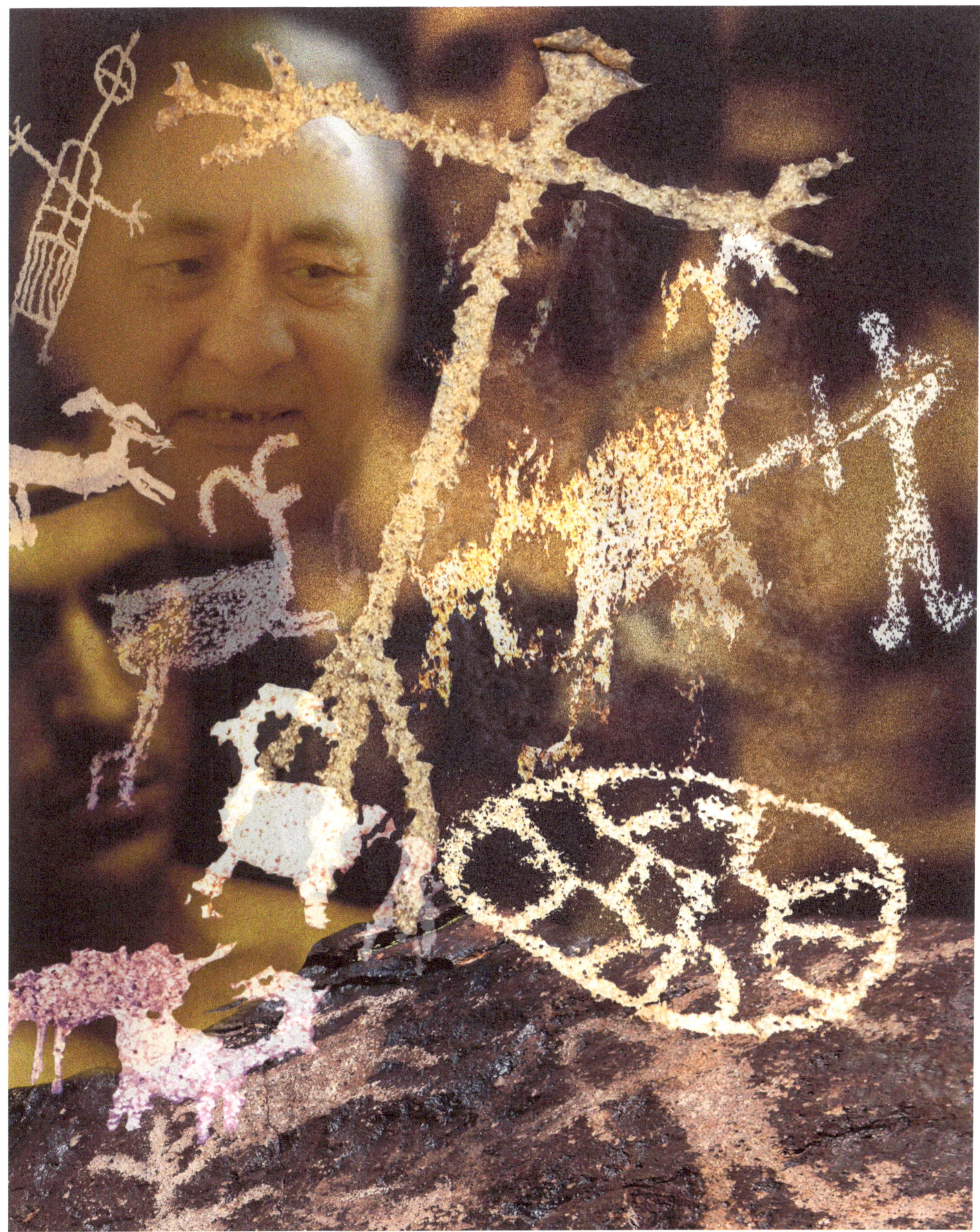

The Struggle Montage — There is nothing good or bad, but thinking makes it so.

The Nature of Evil

Humankind has the capacity of great good and unimaginable evil. Humans choose to believe that good and goodness comes from a pure heart and Godly love and believe that all evil comes from a black heart and the influence of Satan, the god of evil. There is but one God and all that is, comes from the womb of God. A good God cannot create evil nor can an evil God create good. Humankind creates all evil as well as all that is good experienced on Earth.

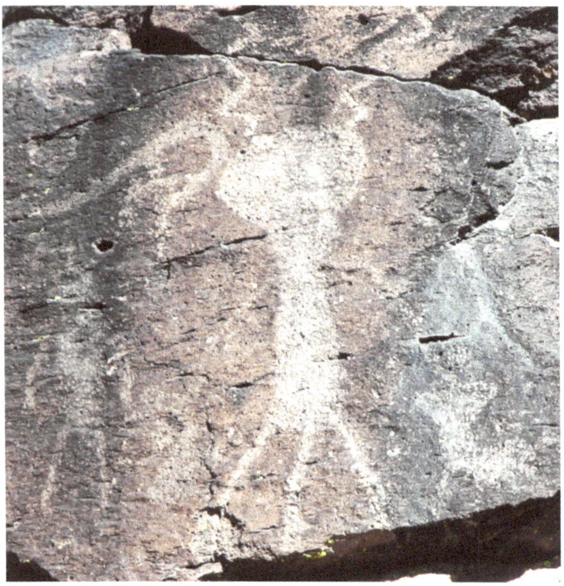

Early European settlers used shotguns to destroy petroglyphs that they called the Devil art up until 1950's.

The human spirit when manifested in an Earthly life forms, separates from the universal mind we call God. It's in this separated form that humans can create and perceive good and evil. All forms of good and evil on this Earth proceeds from the heart and mind of humankind. God does not create good to flow from the mind of humans nor does a devil lead them astray, though some humans would prefer to believe it so.

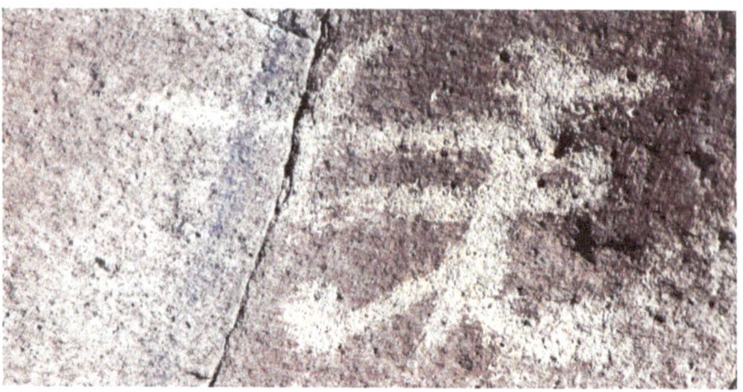

The arrows is nether good or evil it is only a tool.

All the horrendous atrocities visited on humankind were created by humans. The evil that rains on Earth is all human made, but humans would like to blame its origin on an external evil force. The demons and devils that plague humankind are of their own making. Humans own all evil and wicked thoughts, curses and envy, jealousy and hate, cruel and uncivil behavior, and all manner of despot thinking. This negative energy, when filtered through the human being on Earth becomes evil, and when this evil intent is joined with others to achieve political power and physical wealth, it can become extremely powerful, pitting family against family, kingdom against kingdom, nation against nation and religion against religion, the endless struggle. Vanity, it is all vanity.

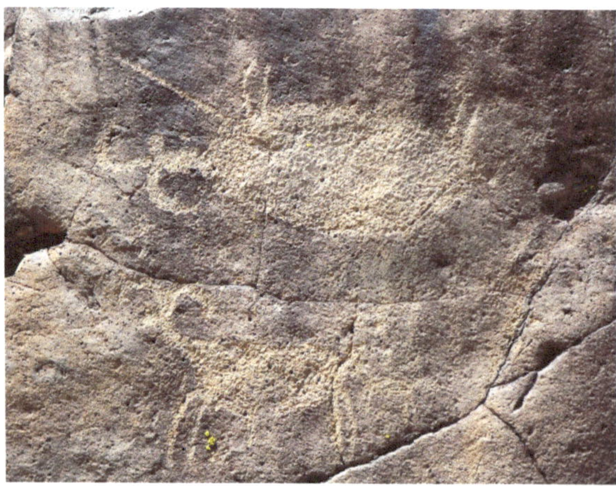

There can be no life without death.

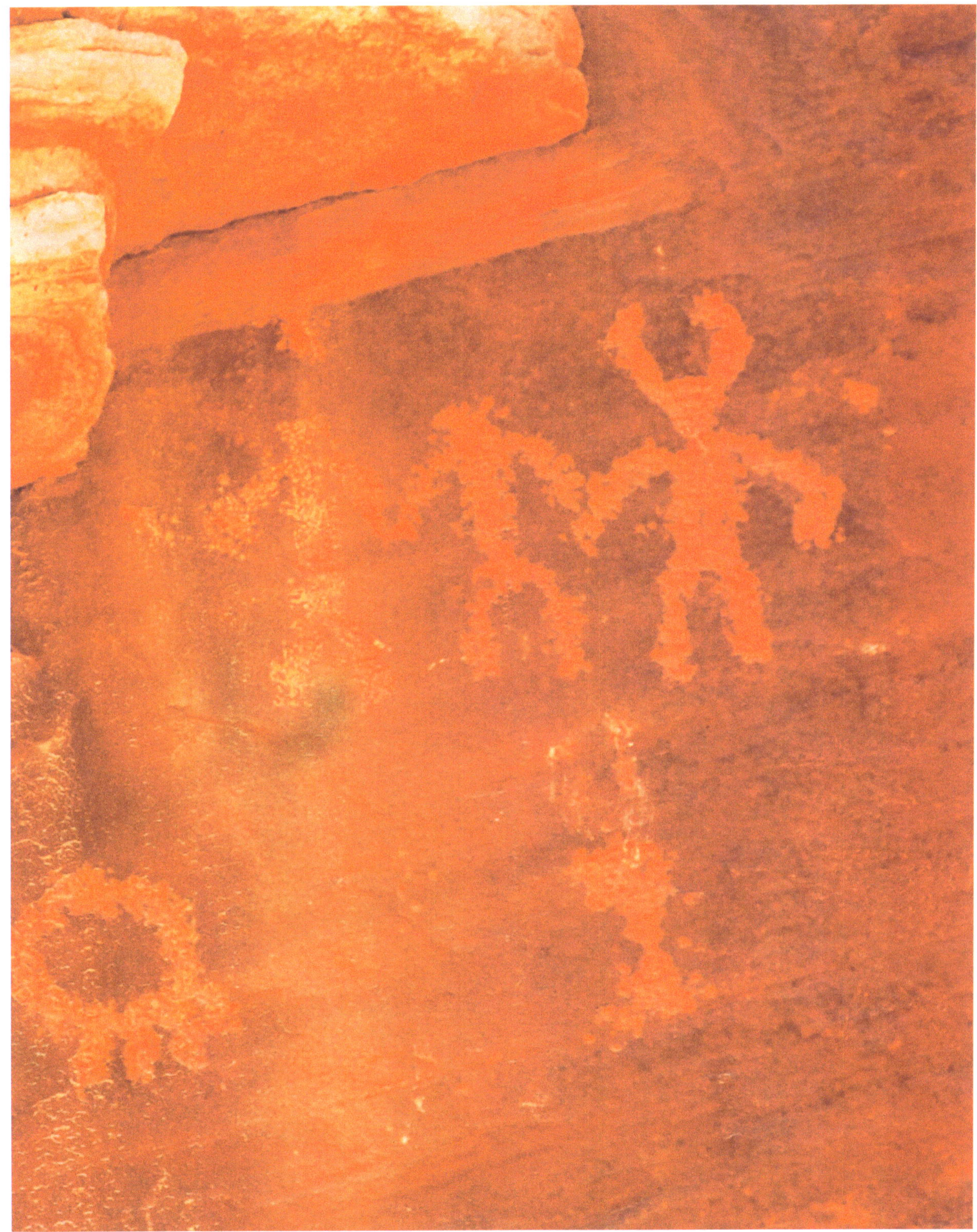

The Earth bound human stands in the middle, hands ever linked between good and evil.

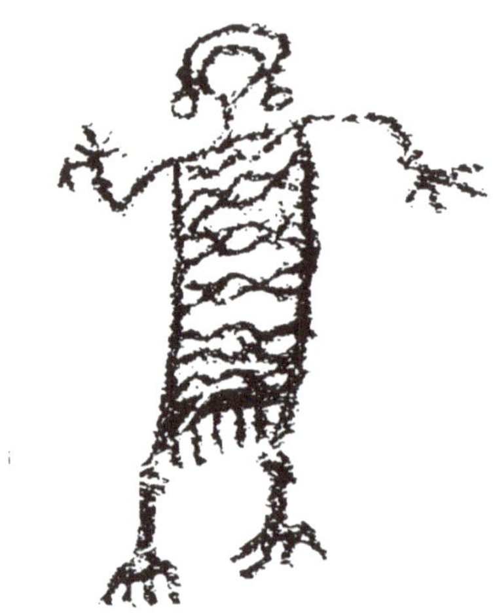

Fear

Deep, I go deep within the Earth now, to the lower world. It is dark. Darkness is all around me. I fear the darkness. I feel the earth begin to tremble. I am more afraid. The earth shakes beneath my feet. What is this I hear? A thumping sounds shatter the silence. I feel the presence coming near. I know it is coming closer, but I cannot see it. I am terrified.

I strain to see in the darkness. Slowly, I recognize shapes, stones, the walls of the boundless cavern. I know that monsters are lurking near. My heart pounds, terror wells up in me and I fall prostrated on the ground in fear. Suddenly I see it, there in the shadow it stands before me. It is gigantic.

I hear a snicker, then a chuckle that becomes a large rolling laugh. Can it be so, this behemoth is laughing at me? I wondered. I raised my head and looked. It stood tall above me. Its body and head were one massive block. Its body is covered with square and rectangular scales with short grasping arms and clawing feet protruding from the massive form, and where its face should be, there is nothing but an undulating glob with its eye perched atop its head. It continued to laugh at me, but I could see no mouth.

"Why do you fear me? Foolish man, have you not chosen to walk this way?"

I could not answer. I could not speak. I prayed this "thing" would leave.

"It is fear," it roared. "It is fear that rules your world. Fear of those that speak a different tongue, for they might speak ill of you and you not know. Fear of those whose skin is of a different color because they might think you odd. Fear of those that believe and practice a different Faith, for they might be right and you wrong. Foolish man, you allow yourself to be ruled by fear."

I knew what it said was true and I hated it for saying so. "Go away, go away, go away," I whispered to the dirt.

"When you cry, don't all humans cry in the same tongue? When you bleed, is not all human blood red? And when you cry out to God, does not but One God hear? Stand foolish man and face your fear."

I stood slowly, cowering lifting not my eyes. When, with heart pounding, I looked up, I could not help laughing. There the monster stood half as tall as my knee. How could I let such a little thing become so large?

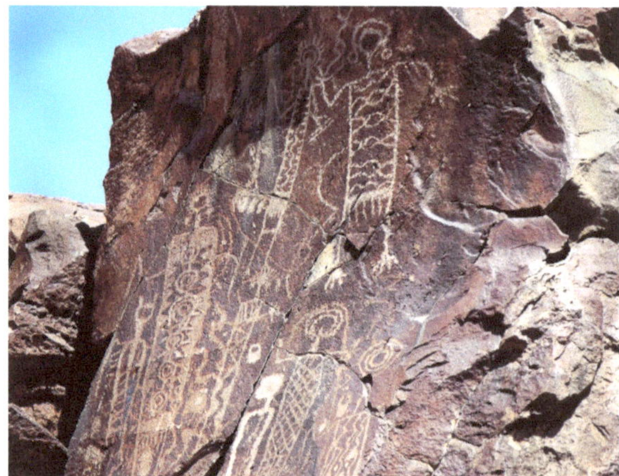

Perspective can change our point of view. If one allows it, the monster of fear can rule our life.

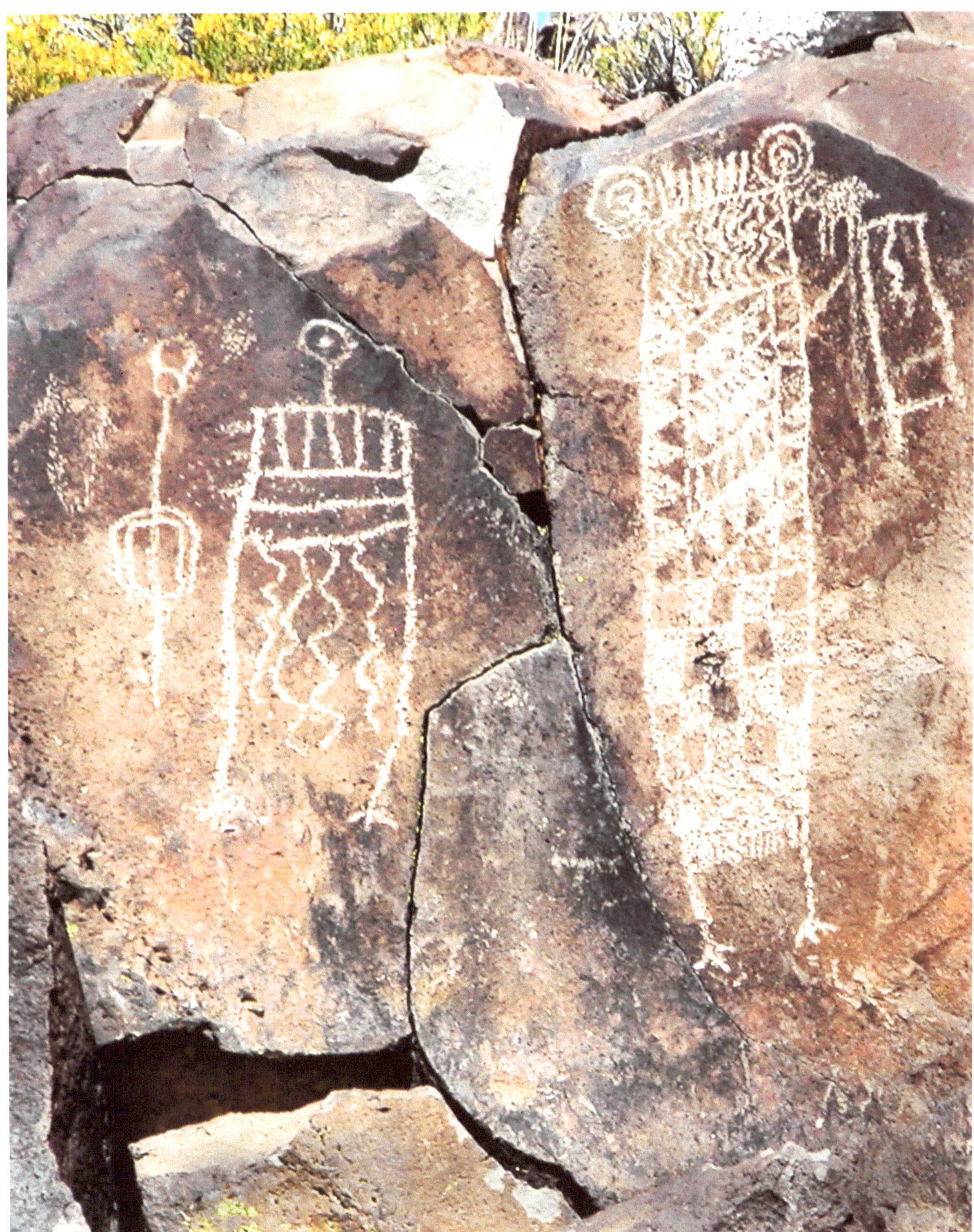

The fear of the unknown is the greatest fear we will ever face.

Found Medicine

I turned and was no longer in the cave, but high above the Earth. I could see people scurrying about their daily lives. Some were living happy lives with family and friend and other were in despair; locked in prisons or fighting useless wars or fighting their own demons of sickness. Each so caught up in their own life they could not see that everyone faced the same trials and tribulations.

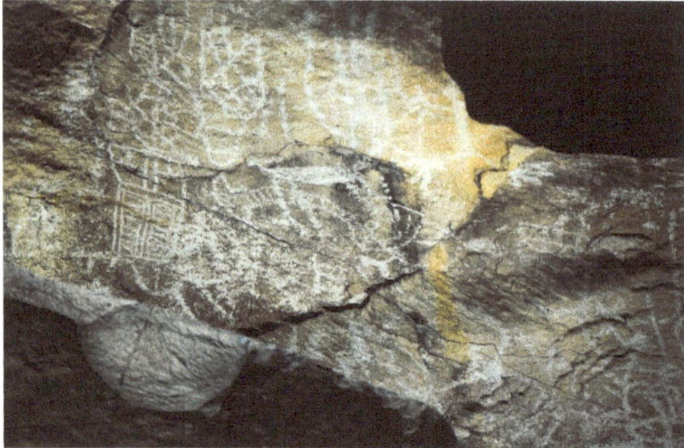

Everyone face the same trials and tribulation only with a different appearance .

When a spirit incarnate in a human form for a life on one of many Earths in the universe, it is to experience physical life at the stage of cultural, technical and emotional development of that Earth. It is only in the physical world of planetary life that we can experience good and evil, joy and sadness, birth and death and the fullness of self. When we once again shed the flesh and return to the Godhead, we return with the knowledge and experiences gained by a life lived. The paradox is we are alone when on this Earth, but not alone in the universe.

Look at the night sky. Are we alone?

If you live away of the glare of city lights, you can see billions of stars at night, yet this is only a fraction of the stars in the universe. Trillions of suns, many with solar systems much like our own, with millions, maybe billons of Earths. We are not alone, yet we are isolated on this planet by an impenetrable physical barrier of distance. However the Shaman, through the process of journeying can pass beyond physical bounds of distance and time and visit these other Earths. This is not a journey of fleshly self, but of spirit. There are no spaceships or teleportation devices, just as there is no time, they travel the vast distances of space entirely without mechanical devises.

Shamans on this Earth can visit out there, and though limited, they may even make contact with other humankind. Some may look strangely like us and other my simple look strange, very strange. Likewise there are others, Shaman visitors from other Earths, visiting here the same way. One might see them as strange light in the night sky, believing they are extraterrestrial space ships. These visitors may make contact with those that are not Shaman and even take them on journeys. They are called UFOs and ET's, but they are like us, beings reaching out trying to understand the fullness of the universe.

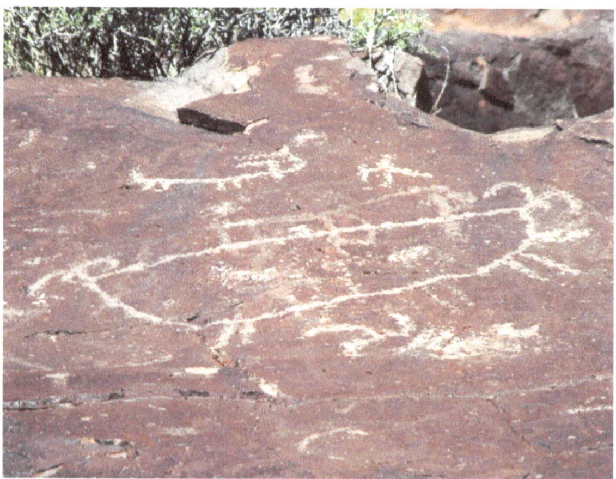

Drawing of a two-headed sheep as some believe or is it a spaceship? The laws of physics keep our bodies bound to this Earth, but the ageless, timeless, boundless human spirit can travel the universe.

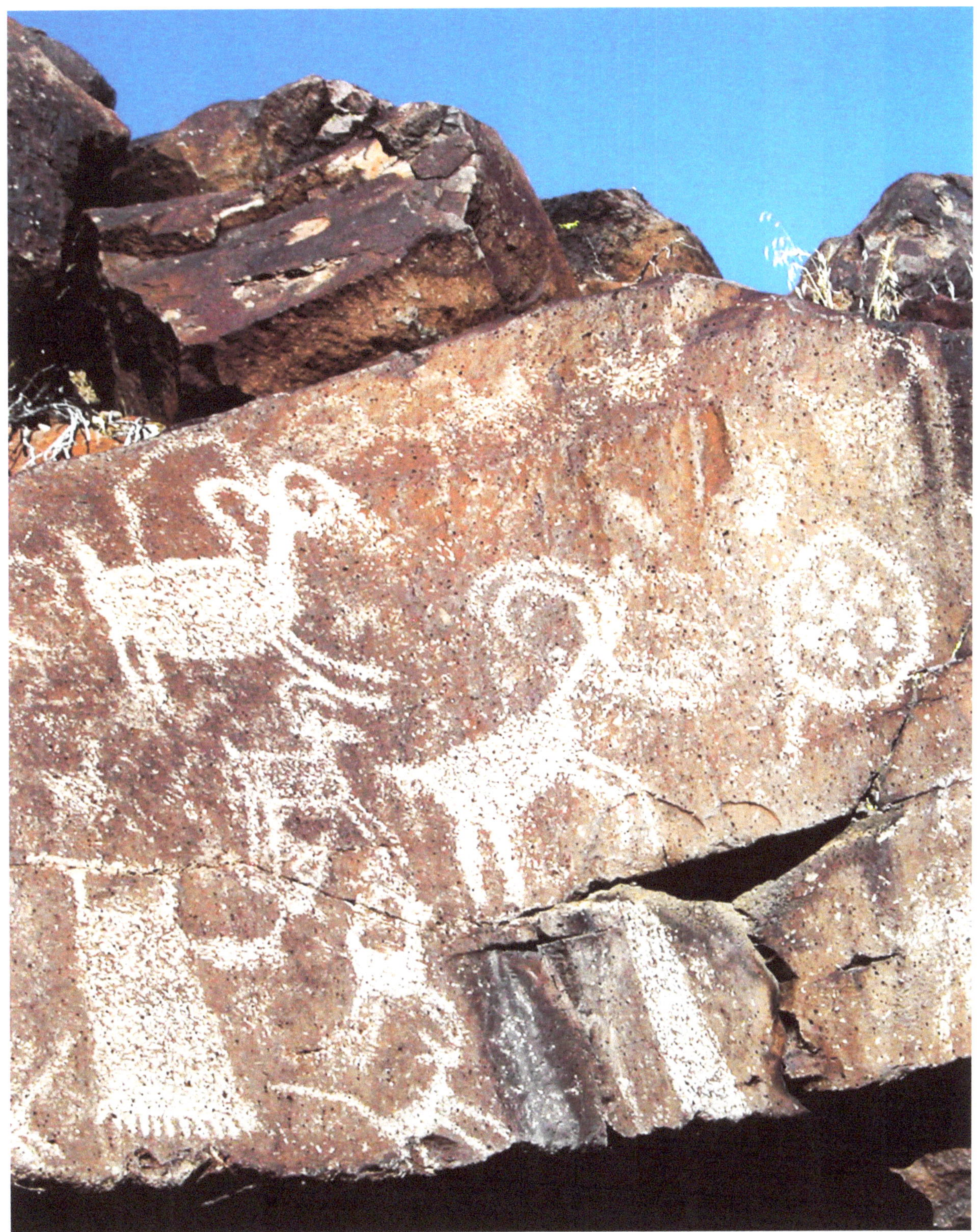

Sheep and cougars are depicted among medicine bundles and shields, travelers all in the universe of the spirit.

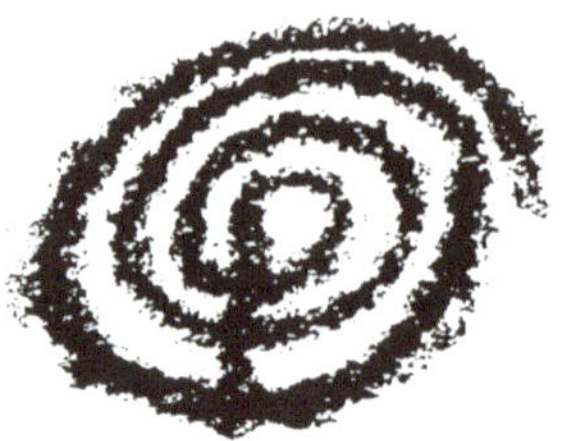

Embracing Good

The King of Kings can be a despot, while the humblest of servants can bring healing to the nations. Everything has a positive and negative, good and bad. What saves lives can kill, and what kills can and does save lives. In the struggle of life, the more one embraces the positive, good, the greater their happiness. By embracing the positive a person can turn that which may appear bad or evil to others, into blessing.

No one can be totally positive, or for that matter totally negative, but they can strive to embrace either the positive or negative. There are those that teach that humankind is born in sin and is therefore by nature evil and that only by following their prescribed method or divine path, can they be saved from damnation. The truth is, God is within each living human being and therefore the nature of God, is within every human. There is no heavenly reward for doing good or damnation for doing evil. We create our own heaven and hell and may dwell in either or both simultaneously. Humankind does not need a priest, taskmaster, monitor, king or government to tell them what is good or evil, the Devine, the God within, if followed, will guide them.

Humans are not good because they do good. They do good, create acts of kindness, feed the hungry, nurse the sick, love their enemies and live just lives, because they are good. To be good, one must simply embrace good, likewise, when humankind allow the negative to rule their live, selfish acts of evil follow. The manifestations of good and evil on Earth are born in the hearts of humankind. The will of humanity must learn to embrace the good and fear not the evil. Morality cannot come from any external force, be it laws, doctrines or leaders, nor can the most despicable acts of evil be attributed to the devil.

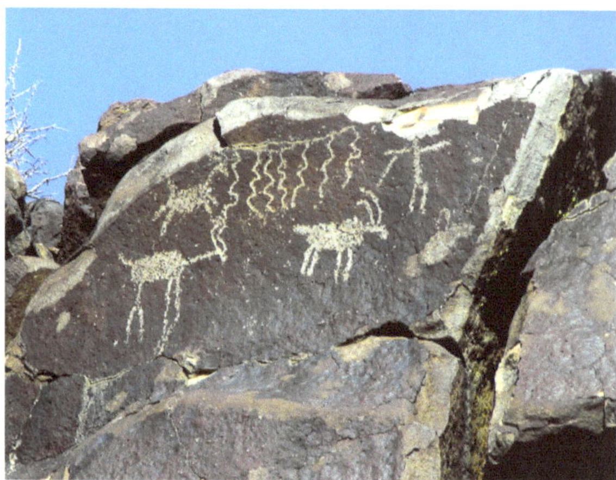

The rain, blessings, fall on the just and the unjust, choosing to do what is right is its own reward.

Rain drops wake me, in the distance I hear the rumble of a thunderstorm that has crossed the mountains and is bringing a pleasant, cooling and refreshing rain. I feel joy in what my journey revealed. Can the fury of nature be called evil? Hurricanes, tornados, earthquakes, tsunamis, fire or flood, are they evil? No, they are what they are, neither good nor evil, but part of what makes life possible on this Earth. Embrace the good that comes your way and turn that which you perceive as evil into life changing opportunities to grow and experience life to the fullest.

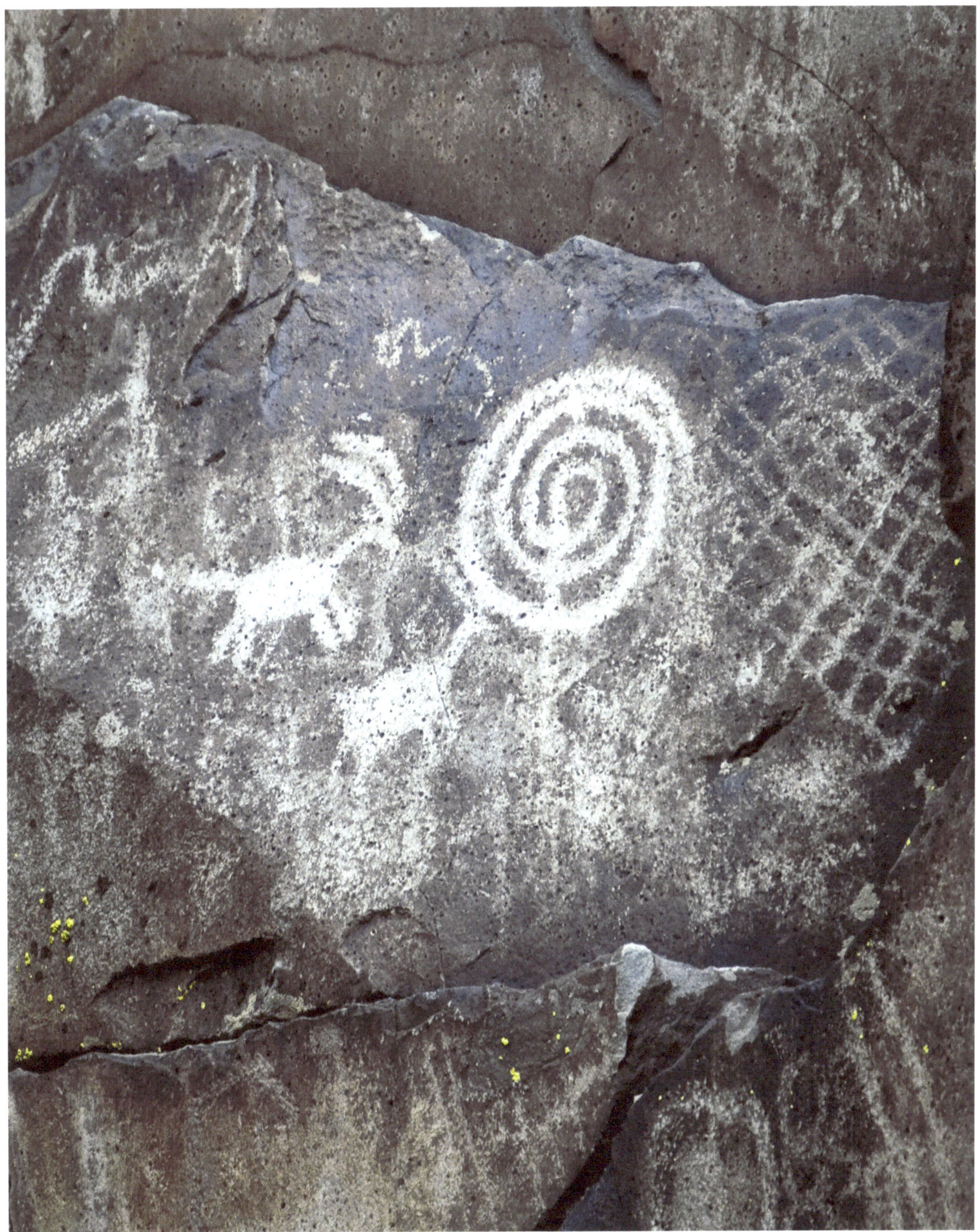

The spiral is the symbol of both the spirit and the spiritual journey.

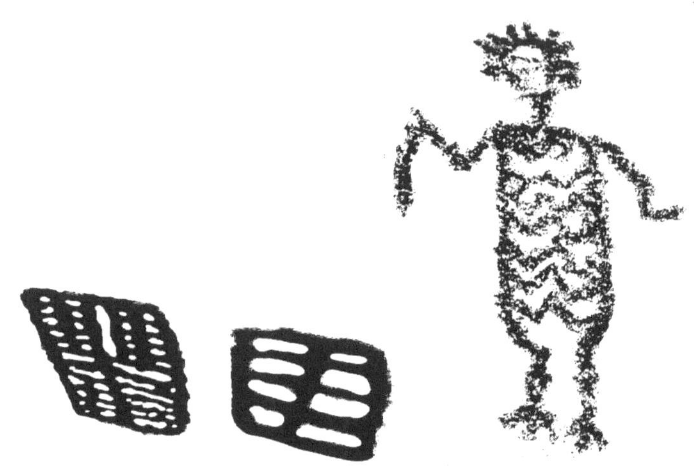

The Triumphant Return

The way of the Shaman is long, and filled with many pitfalls, snares and traps. A Shaman must battle two worlds, the physical and the spiritual. In the physical world, they are often scorn by family, have few if any friends and are feared and deemed a threat by religious organization. In general they are suspect because of their uncanny intuition that often places them on the fringe of society and they are seen as strange, dangerous or possibly deranged. From the time a Shaman is called, there are many distractions, family, community and civil obligation, work, home, finances, sex and even the most mundane requirements of food and shelter are sometimes formidable barrier in successfully becoming a Shaman.

In the spiritual realm the way of the Shaman, takes them down a path where they must face their greatest fears and experience death to self, where they see themselves die, and their bones stripped of flesh, tossed aside and carried off by birds and beasts of the field. Once the Shaman experience total spiritual destruction, they are reassembled, restored, resurrected and returned triumphantly to their world to serve.

The born anew Shaman, the hero with a thousand faces, returns to his or hers community and though they walk in the spirit they must live in the flesh. They are still of this Earth and face its often harsh physical rules, experience the same adversities, angers, prejudice, wants and needs shared by all. The Shaman knows they are neither better nor less than others because of their experience, they are simply different. This difference makes life on Earth a little more difficult and frustrating for the Shaman and annoying to those around them.

The triumphant Shaman is more often feared then respected. Like any human, a Shaman can use their knowledge and abilities for positive or negative, good or evil. A Shaman that chooses to embrace the dark side can wreak havoc for a time, but the laws of the universe will eventually turn their negative energies back upon themselves. Self-distraction is a torturous end worst than can be inflicted by others. Pity the fool on the road of self-destruction.

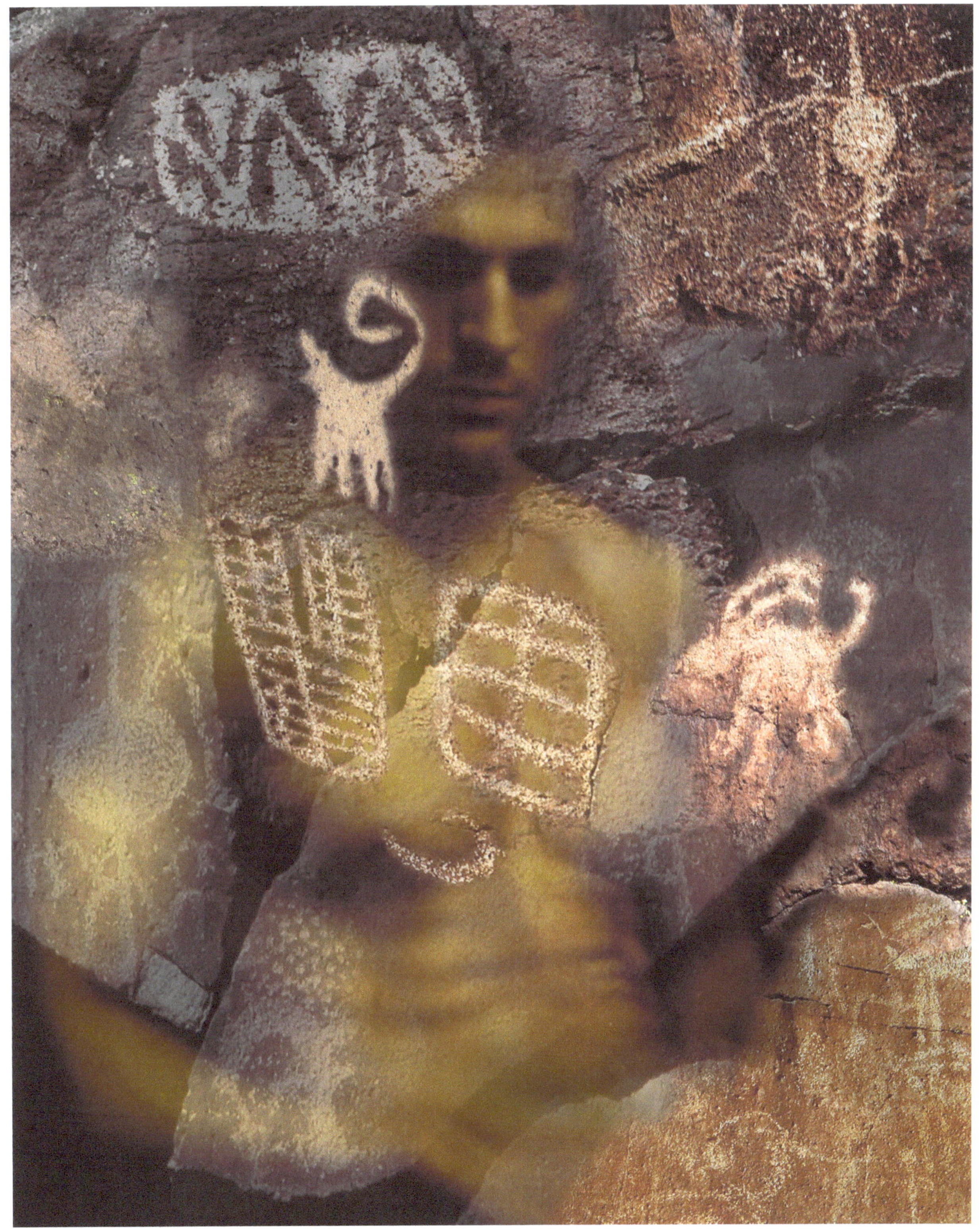

The Triumphant Return Montage — The Shaman after doing battle in the spirit returns to his people .

The Returning Shaman

I made an image of my spirit self on the cave wall and sat to contemplate it. Now I am Shaman, on my shoulder are many responsibilities. To my people I am a spiritual leader. What does that mean? All I know is that I know nothing. The more I think about the vastness of the universe the smaller I become. How can I speak of a God that is unknowable? How can I explain all is one, everything is connected? How can I show the world that I am spirit? I laugh at my foolish wonderings; all I can be is who I am.

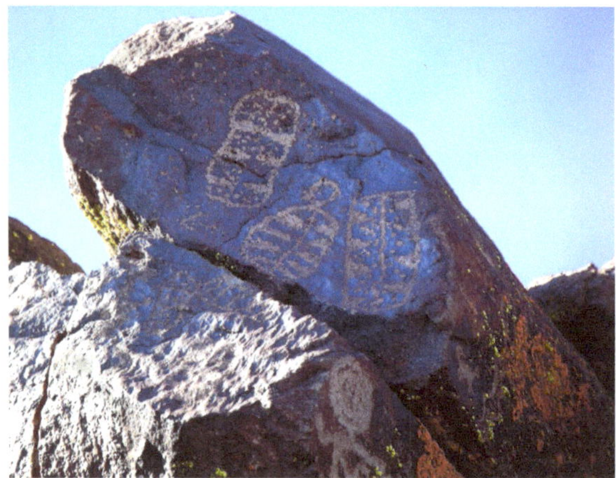

The Shaman make their mark high on the canyon not to show the world who they are, but to remind themselves of the journeys they have made.

On my Journeying I can see the green meadows filled with game, the pinion tree ripe with nuts, the oak laden with its harvest. I can point the way to abundance and tell of dangers, but the people must choose to listen. They say, "The old fool sits in the darkness of his cave, what can he see, and what can he know. He no longer has the strength to hunt. He is old and weak and cannot gather and carry baskets of nuts and acorns. What value is he? Why should we have to share our food with him?"

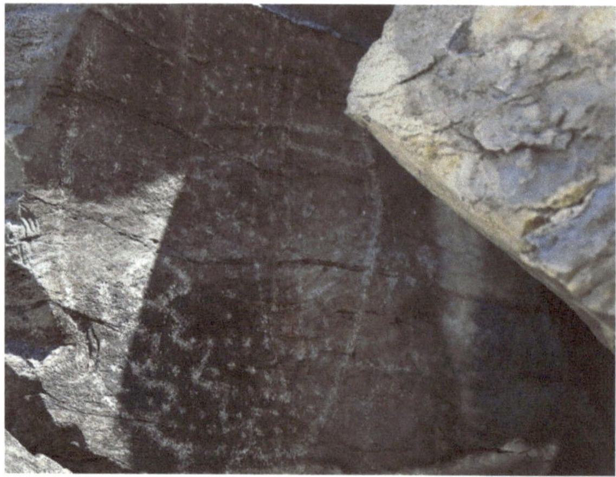

Entry to a Shaman's cave mark by symbols of who occupies it. A Shaman may posses a cave but never own it.

The value of the Shaman is only known to those who recognize it. The community that forgets the value of their Shaman is a community without a vision and doom to a sad end.

Now I can only make my image on the wall of my cave, I am too old to travel to the sacred canyon. I look at my image on the wall and laugh. I know who I am. The fool comes to my cave and points to my image on the wall and asks, "What is that you have painted on the wall?"

"Why, can't you see," I respond. "It's a Cave Baby." I do not speak of things of the spirit to fools.

I chuckle to myself as the fool walks away thinking he is enlightened and tells the world of his great discovery.

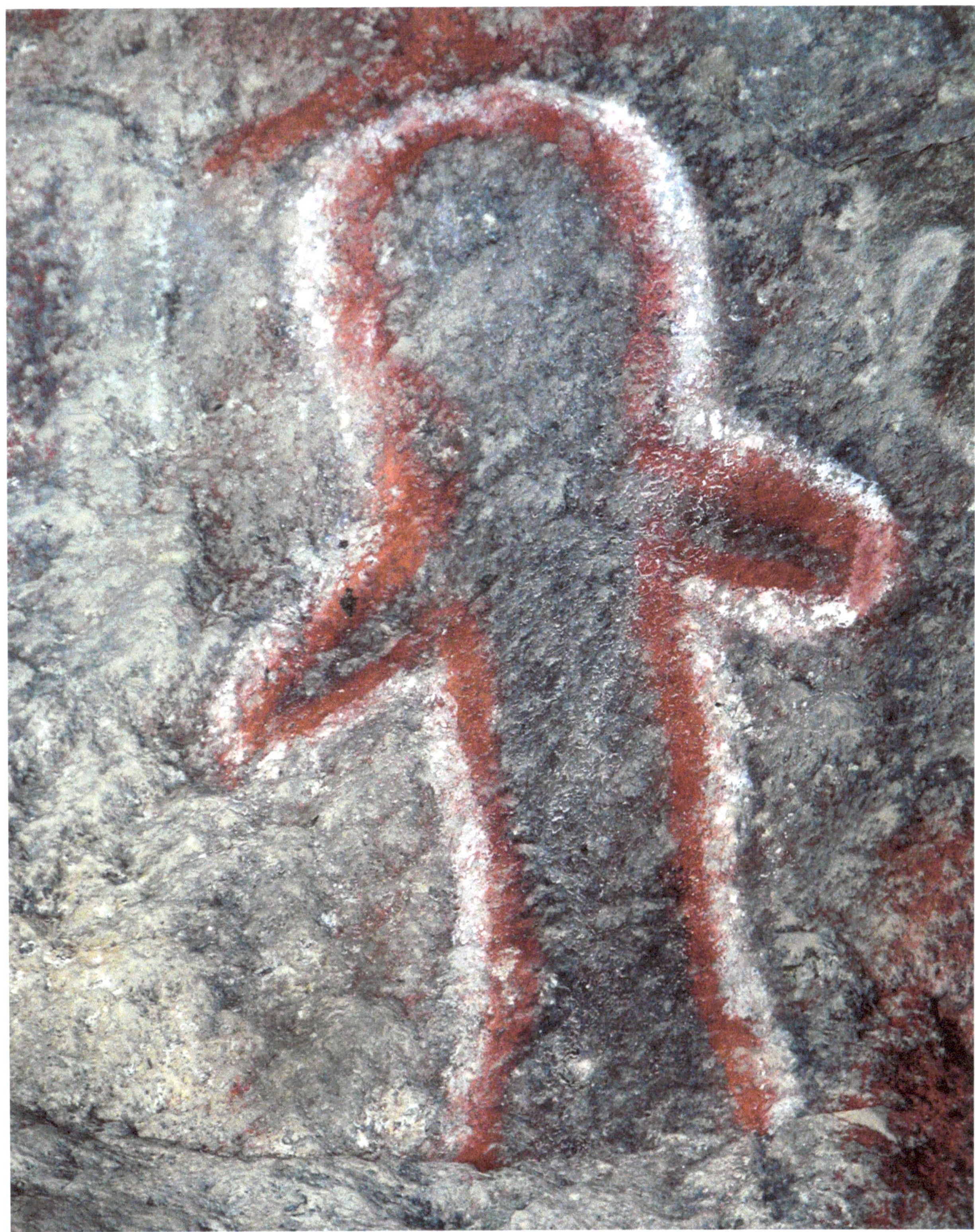

Pictograph of a spirit being painted on the Shaman's wall. It is taboo to speak of a diseased Shaman or identify their image.

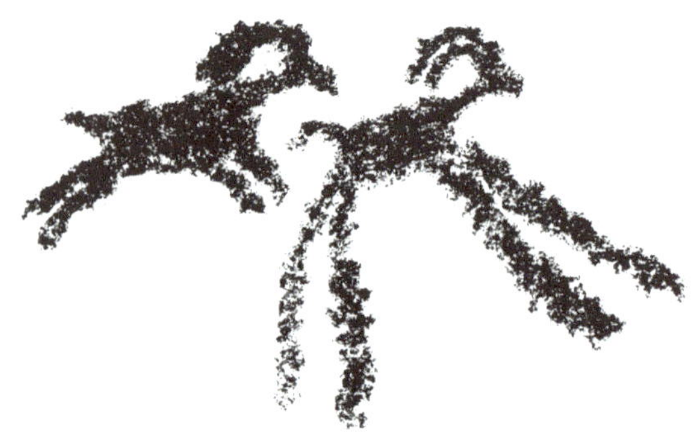

Found Freedom

I am Shaman, I know freedom. I journey, I sore with eagles and ride on clouds, I travel to the edge of the universe and visit the other side, I descend to the lower world filled with wonder and I speak with angles, I see the dance of life and like David the King, I dance naked before God unashamed, I journey, I know freedom.

Like those before me, I share my wisdom in story and parables. Be they scripture or myth, the truth in the scripture or myth is the treasure. Believing the truth of the scripture of myth is the folly.

Jesus said, "and you shall know the truth, and the truth shall make you free."

When a person discovers the truth in the story, sermon, parable, scripture or myth is when they are truly set free. Sacred stories and scripture are always metaphoric, their truth is often veiled requiring the seeker of knowledge to dig deep to find it, as a means of paying a price for that information. However as long as one holds to a belief that their sacred stories and scriptures are literal truths, they are bound to defend them and at the same time never transcend to the truth within them. The Shaman realizes that all myths and scriptures are not to be taken as literal stories of fact, but as vehicle of spiritual truths.

The founders and key figures of all religions claim that their truth will bring freedom, however as the small group of followers grow they some how morph into and oppressive organization with rules and dogma the keep its members bound through fear and the belief that they are the only true religion. Shamanism comes from a firsthand spiritual experience that is liberating and truly has the power to set one free, it is not bound by structure, dogma, religious text or hierarchy.

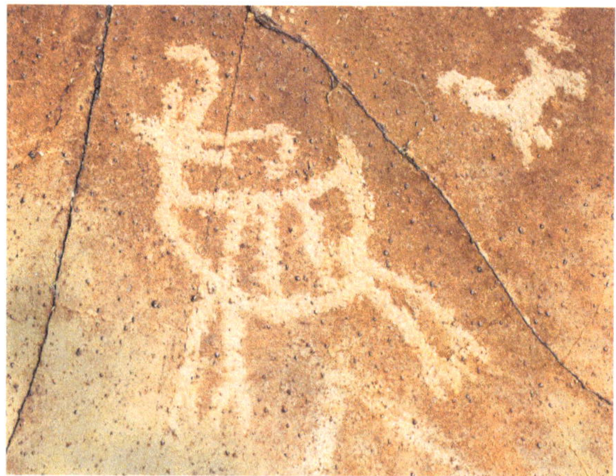

No joy of freedom is greater expressed than by that of bounding sheep. The Shaman express their freedom through the image of bounding sheep, so light on their feet it appears that they could fly.

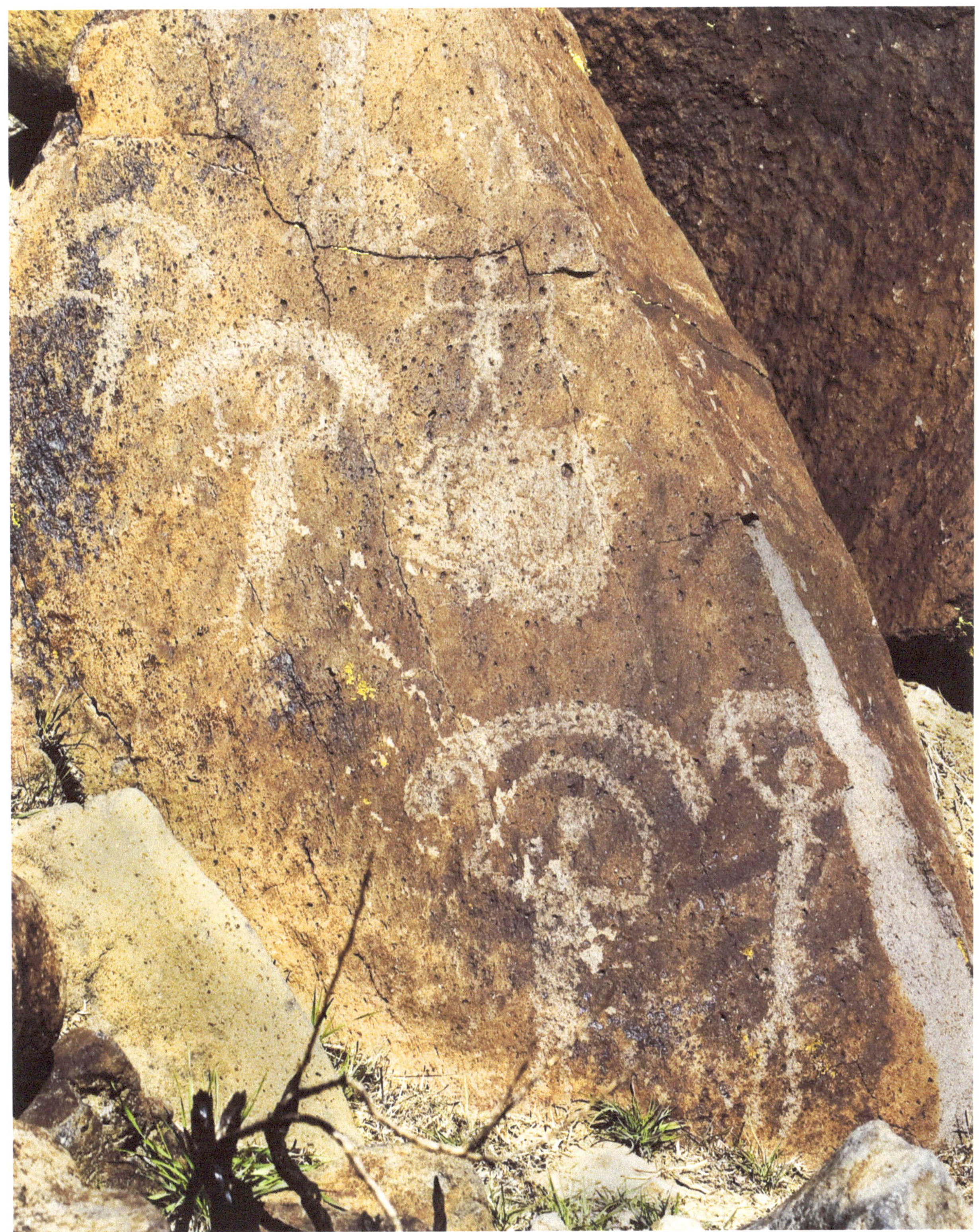

Sky dancers dance with rainbow parachutes by which they slowly descend back to Earth.

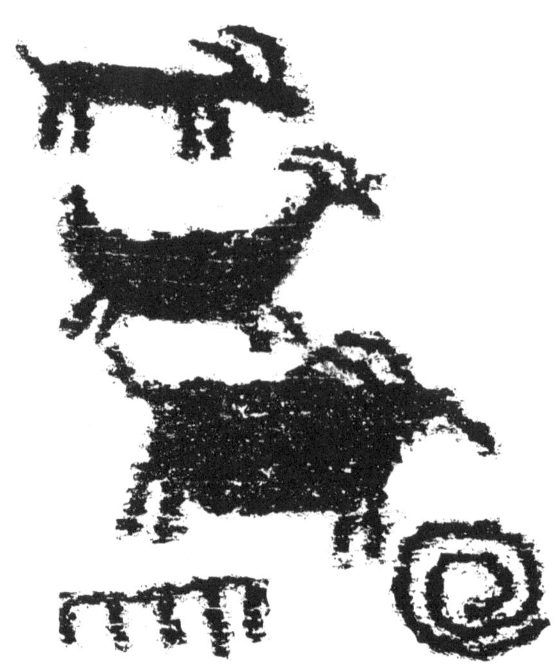

The Storyteller

Today, as in seasons past, the Shaman may be a political leader and/or a spiritual leader, a healer or any combination thereof or simply slip quietly to a mountaintop and become a hermit. There are no two Shaman alike and no prescribe code of practice, but there is one commonality, all Shamans are storytellers. They reach into the dream space, the source of stories and bring them to the Earth. They share their experiences of their journeying in myths and psalms often shrouded them in the clock of parables. Many of the Shaman's of Old's stories are still with us today, from the Shaman King David of the Hebrews; the myths of the Greeks, Lao Tsu of China; Buddha, to the Shaman Jesus of Nazareth; and on through the prophets of the Middle-East; their stories have become revered as sacred writings to their followers. Many of these sacred stories are based on even older myths that had been told for thousands of year around campfires from the very dawn of human civilization.

Myths, the mystical stories are stories of truths, that are truly most effective when told by a storyteller, not read from carefully edited manuscripts. When the myth or parables are told, spoken by a Shaman, it becomes relevant because it is in the moment, alive and now, a living story heard as if for the first time. The source story may be thousands of years old, but when spoken from the heart and mind of a living being, the words, inflections and intonation become relevant to that moment. The words spoke and the words heard exist only in that moment and will never be again. Even if it is captured on paper, film or recording device, the relationship of storyteller, listener and the exact situation, will never be the same. It is like the performance of a live stage play, no two are the same.

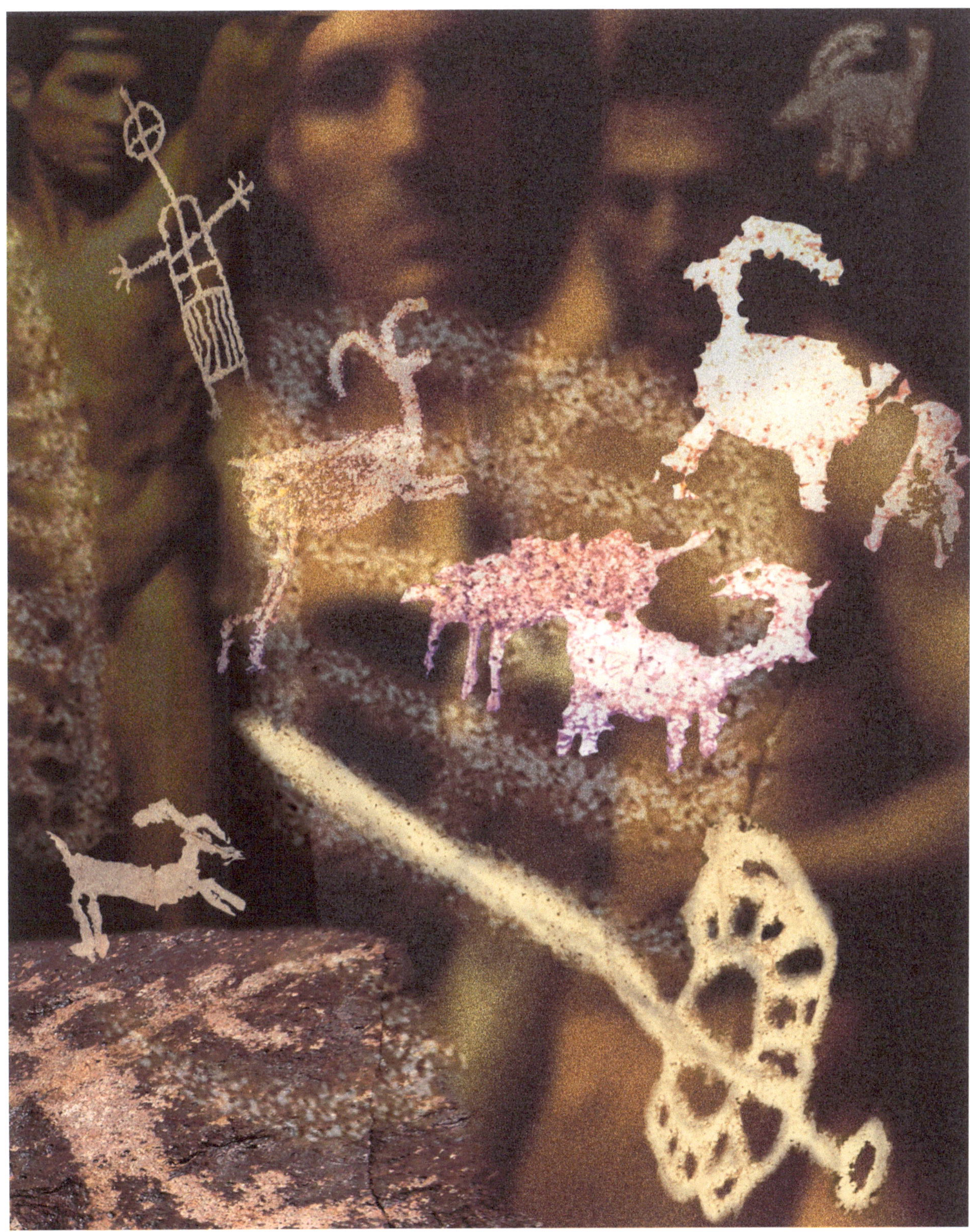

The Storyteller Montage — The Shaman teaches through stories and parables.

Listening to Self

I sat by my fire in my sacred space and prepared to journey. I see before me a small park that appears to be in the heart of a large, busy city. On a bench a familiar figure sits. I realize it's me. Not me of my mirror, but a younger stronger me, the me that I see when my eyes are closed, the real me. I hastily approach and take a seat on the bench, but do not speak, just sit. With purpose the other turns and asks, "Why are you afraid to be alone with yourself?"

"You are the only one that knows the true me." I answered.

"That is true." My inner self answered. "Your fears come not from me knowing the true you, but you knowing the true me. It is much easier to ignore your inner self than face the truth of your reality. It is only I that know the secrets of your heart, your failures and aspirations. You are now a Shaman and must face me in all things. Listen to my voice for it is your true voice, see as I see and feel what I feel, for we are one. I am the part of you that is one with the universe. I am the spirit with in you, the Christ consciousness, the universal mind of God; I am, the I Am in you."

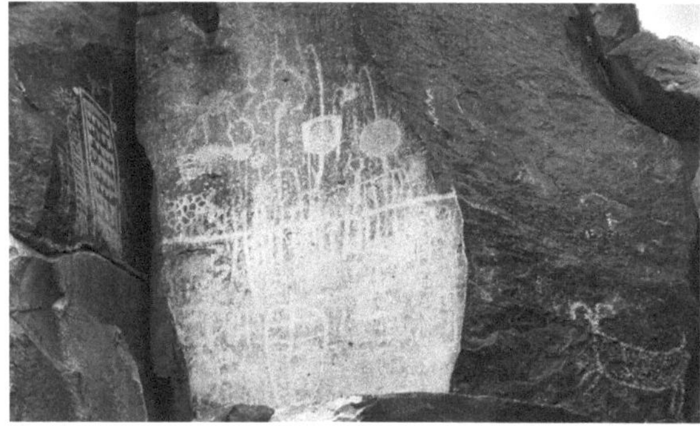

The same stories are written on stone over and over. Shaman's have told their truths in stories and parables for centuries and in all corners of the Earth.

The Story Weaver

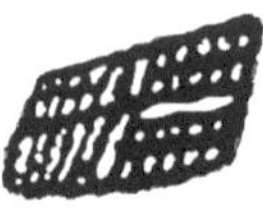

The scene suddenly shifted, before me was a great loom and above it a sign the read, "The Story Weaver." I instantly knew the meaning. The call of the Shaman above all is that of story weaver, and through those stories make known the mysteries of life, the universe and God. The stories of the Shaman may seem simple, for the Shaman often speaks in parables, the wisdom and the truth veiled from the foolhardy, but never from the true seeker. The Shaman Jesus said, "Ask, and it shall be given to you; seek, and you shall find; knock, and is shall be opened. For everyone who asks receives, and he who seeks finds, and to him who knocks it shall be opened."

It is the responsibility of the Shaman to tell the stories, not interpret or explain. Those that have ears to hear will hear and those that do not have ears, will not. It is easier to open a deaf man's ears than to make a fool listen. Likewise be cautious in giving advice too freely, for free advice is perceived as of little value. When someone comes to you for wisdom, watch, listen and be sensitive in the spirit, you will learn their motive, are they truly seeking wisdom or simply asking to have their ears tickled. Be frugal with the knowledge and wisdom given to you, but at the same token, do not line your own purse. The gifts of the spirit cannot be bought or sold.

Weave the stories given you and share them to those that choose to come and listen. Do not be offended if your words fall on deaf ears, it is not your reasonability to make them hear. Though we are all part of this organism we call the universe mind or God, each being is an individual and must work out their own reality.

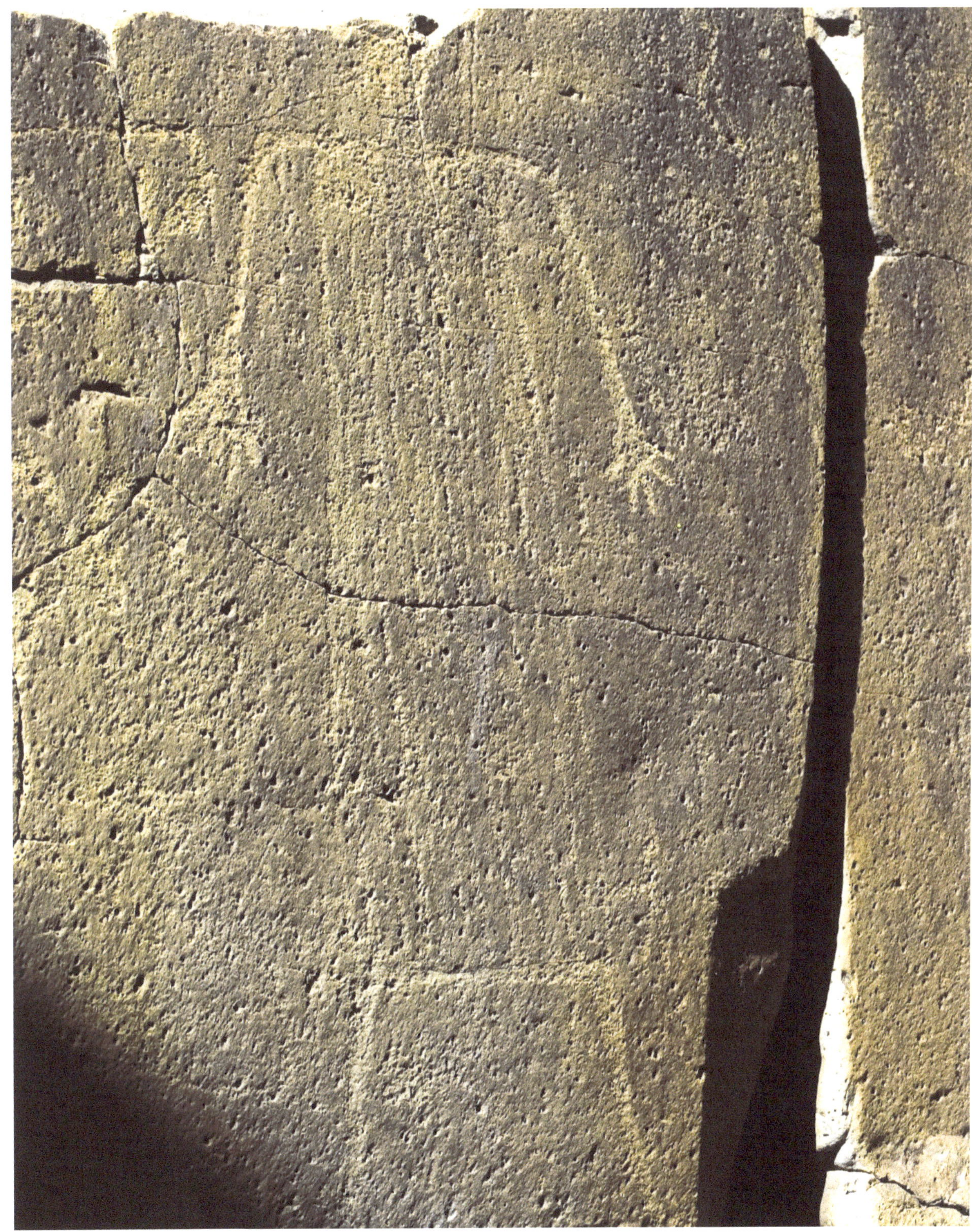

The images, symbols and stories of the Shaman are the same the world over because they speak the same universal truths.

Telling the World

The Shaman is compelled to tell the world of their revelation. They scribe it on the canyon walls over and over, but people are so focused on their own little that world they don't look up to see the answers to that which they seek are written on the walls just above their heads. That which is simple, close at hand and the easiest to understand are always pushed aside for the exotic, the mysterious, that which is impossible to obtain. To love God and your neighbor are the simplest of commandment, yet the hardest to keep because it requires that one must love themselves first. The God in you and your neighbor is the God you must love, nothing more, nothing less.

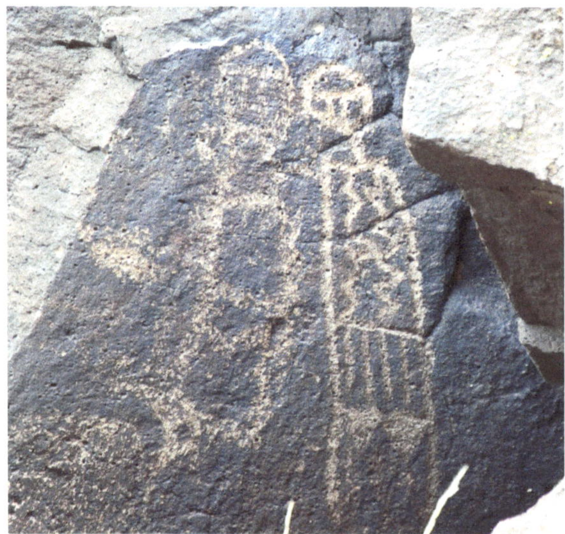

The Shaman brings a massage of religious tolerance to the world today. Will the world listen?

Walk the Walk

The Shaman is compelled to share what they see, learn and know, but this sharing is not evangelistic in nature. The call to Shamanism is a spiritual call not compunction, the message the Shaman brings is for all.

The Shaman knows they must take the beam from their own eye before they try to remove the speck form another. They must learn to balance their lives between the spirit world and natural world. They are of little value to society cloistered on a mountain top. They, like all humans, are in this life to live it, not hide from it. They must learn to control the needs of the flesh, food, sex and wealth in balance with the world around them.

Shamans are doers not just spectators in the process of life. Through the eons they have adapted too many social and economic changes. They have been powerful leaders and despised outcast and have learned to adapt in all situations. Today, in an age of so-called intellectual enlightenment, the world sees religious extremism and intolerance is on the rise. Single-minded fanaticism is ripping apart nations and destroying countries through wars and economic chaos, religious groups denying basic human right to others because they are of a different faith. When will the voice of reason return to this Earth? Maybe voice of the Shaman calling for balance and acceptance will be heard. Let there be hope.

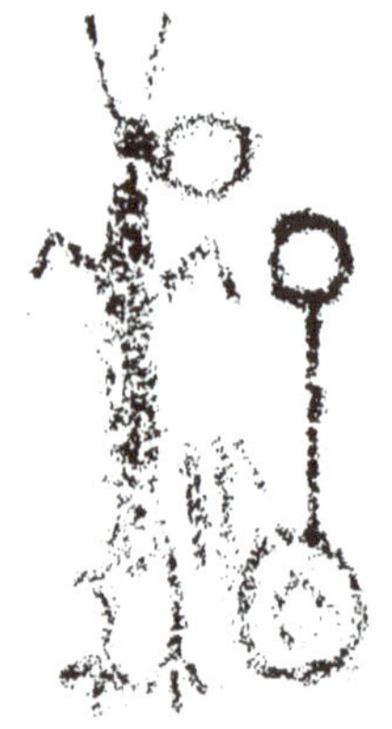

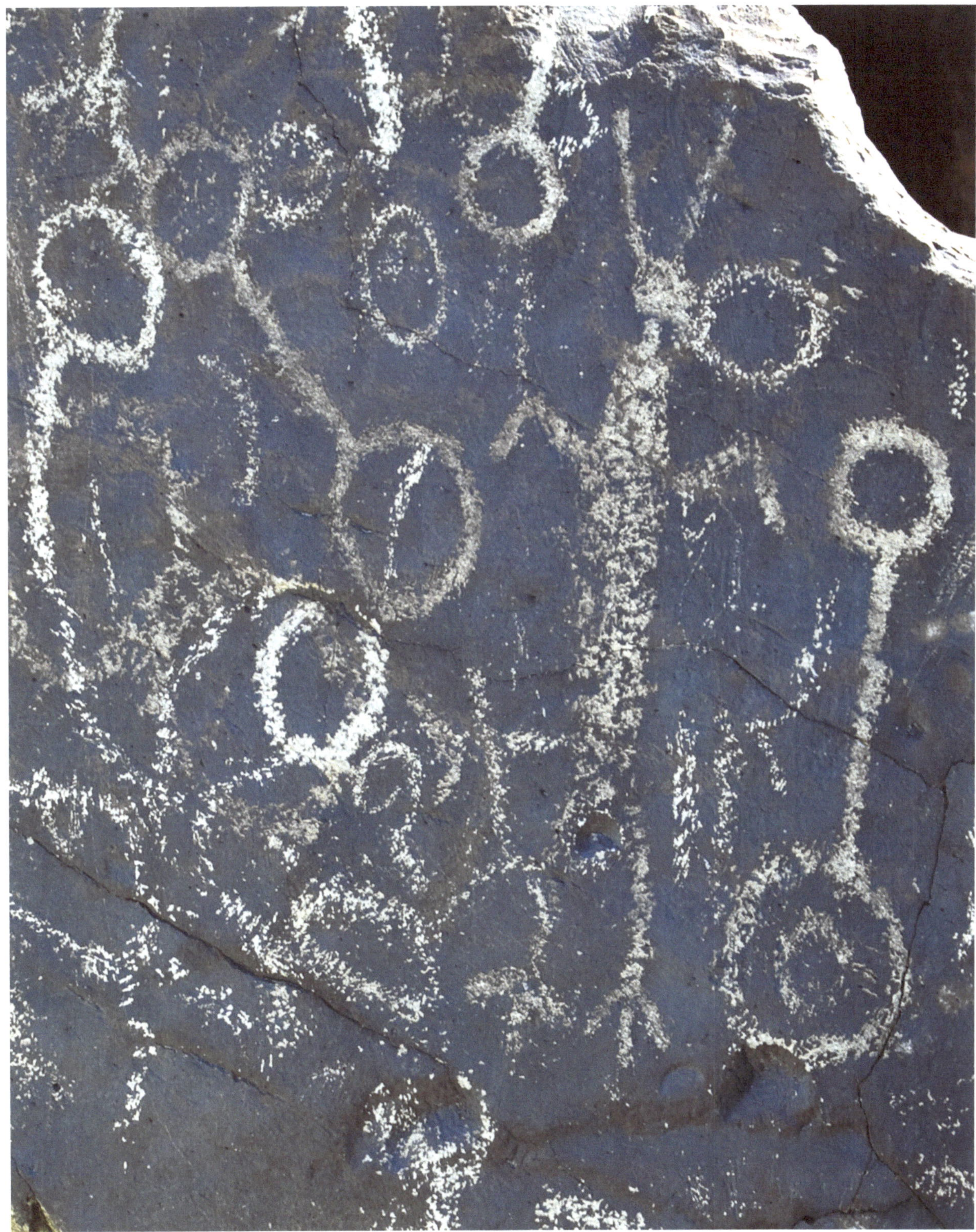

The Shaman is a storyteller telling the stories of the universe to all that will listen.

Tomorrow's Story

The time of the Shaman Returning.

The time of the Shaman is always now. Modern humans may look back at the teaching and art of the past and think how primitive and irrelevant the pecking on stone are compared to our complex world of today. Some of todays major religions believe in an apocalyptic end to Earth brought about by God, and are doing everything in their power to help the end come. There are holy wars raging around the globe using up the Earths limited recourses and killing people in the name of their god. Great nations are deadlocked in ideological battles in their governments tearing themselves apart. Humankind is abusing Mother Earth with total disrespect to the fact She is the source of their survival. Yet in an instant a sun flair, a polar magnetic reversal or climate change can return us all to the Stone Age.

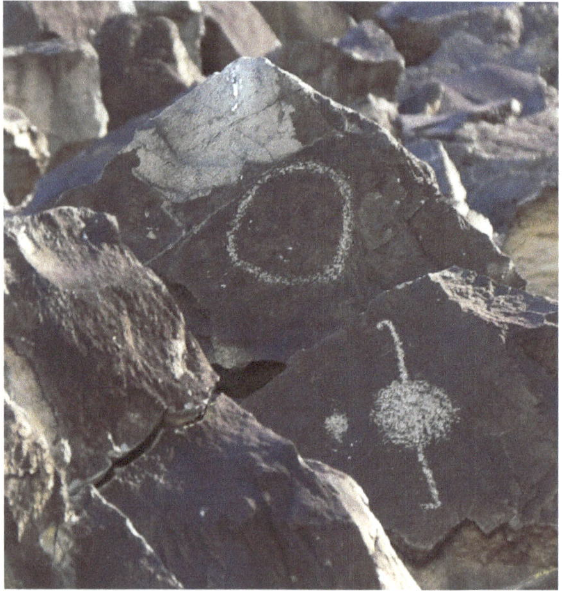

The human mind that speak to us from so long ago is the same mind in us today. When they looked to the heavens what did they see, what did they know?

There a many predictions of doom for this Earth. It will, like all things, someday end and return to cosmic dust. Before then however, there will be many more lifetime spent on this Earth. What is in store? Oh the great and powerful nations of today will decline and fade into distant memories. Religions will battle themselves into destruction then reemerge and start the whole process over. Life on this Earth will ebb and flow and someday a long, long time from now we will all return to the Godhead to realize we were a part of It all of the time.

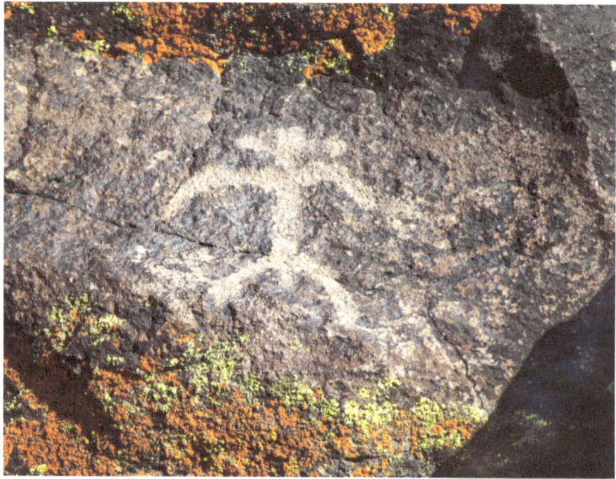

We all experience joy and fear, we crave love and acceptance and we all want peace and security. We are social beings, but in the end we all stand alone and must work out our own salvation.

Although the Shaman appears to stands alone, he or she has journeys through time and space and taps the wisdom of the ages. They learned that God, that so many desperately seek, already dwells in each of us.

Tomorrow's story is the same as yesterday's, only told by someone new. There is only one reality, the NOW. Learn the simple truths the Shaman brings to the Earth. Life on this Earth is fragile, very fragile and temporal, the spirit is eternal, without time, only NOW.

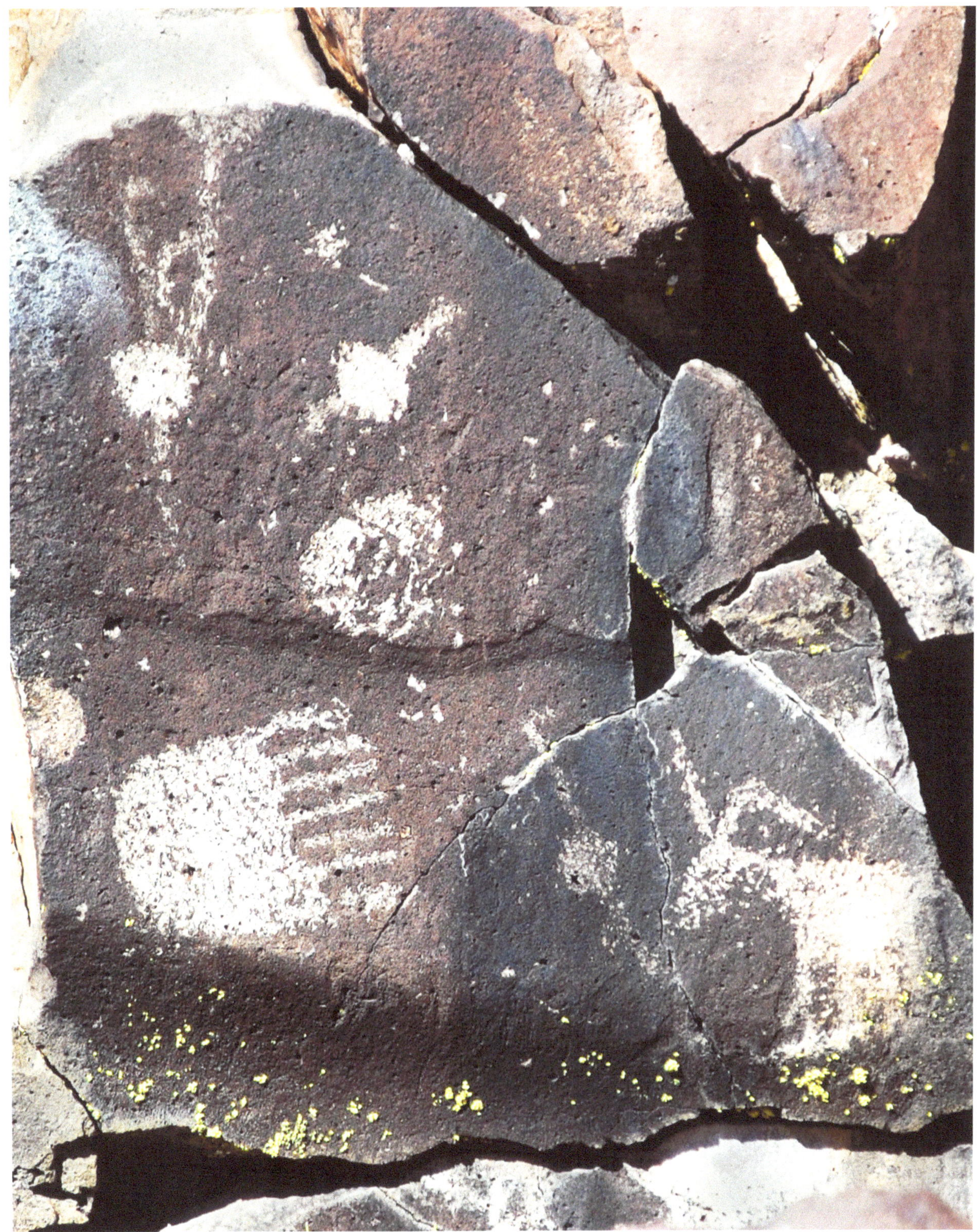

Images from the cosmos, sign of knowledge of the universe and solar systems from afar or simple imaginings? You be the judge.

Photo Information

All photographs in this book were take by the author using Nikon digital cameras and Nikon Nikkor lenses, in a raw format. They were processed with Adobe Photoshop and converted to JPAG files for inclusion in this book.

9; Details of a repeatedly used ceremonial rock in Little Petroglyph Canyon, CA.

11; Single Shaman panel in Little Petroglyph Canyon, CA.

13; Abstract image that represent ideas on a panel in in Little Petroglyph Canyon, CA.

15; Animal guide panel in Valley of Fire, NV.

17; Life size Shaman stands guard at rock craves in Little Petroglyph Canyon, CA.

18; Shamanism is not restricted to a specific gender, this petroglyph in Little Petroglyph Canyon, CA, is a very feminine figure.

20; Headdress are a common part of the Shaman's attire, using feathers antler and woven fiber. This photo of a Shaman from Little Petroglyph Canyon, CA, shows an elaborate headdress.

21; The central Shaman in this photo high in Little Petroglyph Canyon, CA, show's a strange to an ET Gray.

22a; A popular area for petroglyphs in Little Petroglyph Canyon, CA.

22b; Close-up of a zigzag petroglyph in Little Petroglyph Canyon, CA.

23; Detail of a logo pattern from Valley of Fire, NV.

24a; Lenticular clouds photographed near Tehachapi, CA using an infrared filter.

24b; Deeply etched sheep from Little Petroglyph Canyon, CA.

25; Carved logo in a possible timeline from Little Petroglyph Canyon, CA.

26; Panel of two Shaman images in Little Petroglyph Canyon, CA.

27; Details of a Shaman from Little Petroglyph Canyon, CA.

30; Three sheep panel in Little Petroglyph Canyon, CA.

31; A Shaman and hunter follow a sheep in Little Petroglyph Canyon, CA.

33; Most photographed panel of Shaman in Little Petroglyph Canyon, CA.

34a; Sheep and medicine bags high on a cliff in Little Petroglyph Canyon, CA.

34b; Petroglyph resembling the Yen/Yang symbol from Little Petroglyph Canyon, CA.

35; A wheel symbol from Valley of Fire, NV.

36a; Hunter killing a sheep from Little Petroglyph Canyon, CA.

38a; Large headed three legged Shaman from Little Petroglyph Canyon, CA.

38b; Hunter detail from Little Petroglyph Canyon, CA.

38c; Dead sheep from panel in Little Petroglyph Canyon, CA.

39; Detail from Valley of Fire, NV.

40; Multiple Shaman on a panel in Little Petroglyph Canyon, CA.

41; Fearsome Shaman from a panel in Little Petroglyph Canyon, CA.

42a; Cave panel, Little Lake, CA.

42b; Controversial two-headed sheep panel from Little Petroglyph Canyon, CA.

43; Panel detail from Little Petroglyph Canyon, CA.

44; Rain panel in Little Petroglyph Canyon, CA.

45; Spiral from Little Petroglyph Canyon, CA.

48a; Medicine shield panel, Little Petroglyph Canyon, CA.

48b; Shield detail form Little Petroglyph Canyon, CA.

49; Pictograph from Creation Cave, Tomo-Kahni site, Tehachapi, CA.

50; Detail from Little Petroglyph Canyon, CA.

51; Dancer panel, Little Petroglyph Canyon, CA.

54; Detail from Little Petroglyph Canyon, CA.

55; Shaman panel from lower Little Petroglyph Canyon, CA.

56; Two Shaman, Little Petroglyph Canyon, CA.

57; Detail from Little Lake, CA, panel.

58a; Detail, Little Lake, CA.

58b; Shaman, Little Petroglyph Canyon, CA.

59; Detail, Little Petroglyph Canyon, CA.

Shaman Art Information

The black and white art used in this book is taken directly form photograph of the petroglyph to preserve the feel, texture and style of the art and artist.

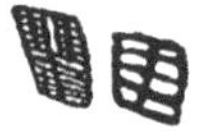

5; Medicine shields, a form of logo or Shaman signature.

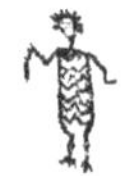

6; Shaman, with a feminine form.

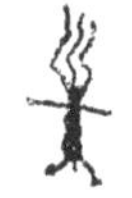

10; Shaman with spick headdress of the three words.

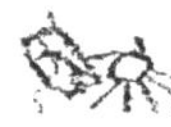

12; Sun and sky logo.

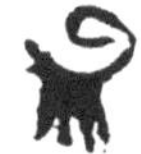

14; Cat or cougar, with its long curving tail.

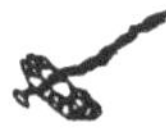

18; Atlatl, a throwing stick used before bows, also a phallic symbol.

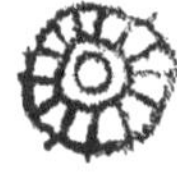

20; Medicine wheel often used to represent the cycle of life.

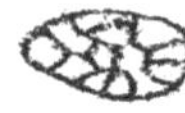

22; Misshaped medicine wheel, a sign of disharmony.

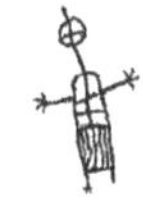

26; Shaman with a face of the four directions of Earth.

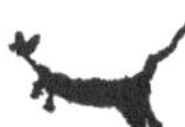

28; Leaping cat or cougar, with its long but straighter tail.

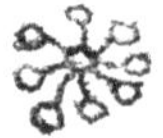

34; Medicine shields, often indicating a balanced life to the Shaman .

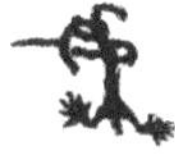

36; Hunter with bow, an emblem of hunter magic.

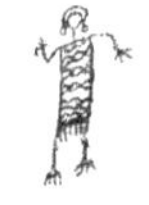

40; Shaman with eagle feet in a stocking or fearful pose.

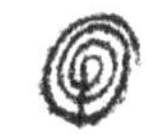

44; A spiral, the symbol of spirit and life's journey.

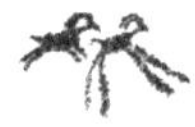

50; Leaping bighorn sheep and sign of good fortune, food and rain.

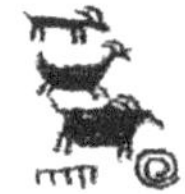

52; Three sheep with emblems, a mark of the storyteller.

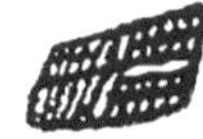

54; A woven pattern medicine shield.

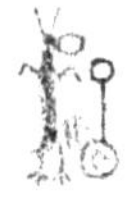

56; A Grasshopper Shaman telling the world the stories of life.

Index

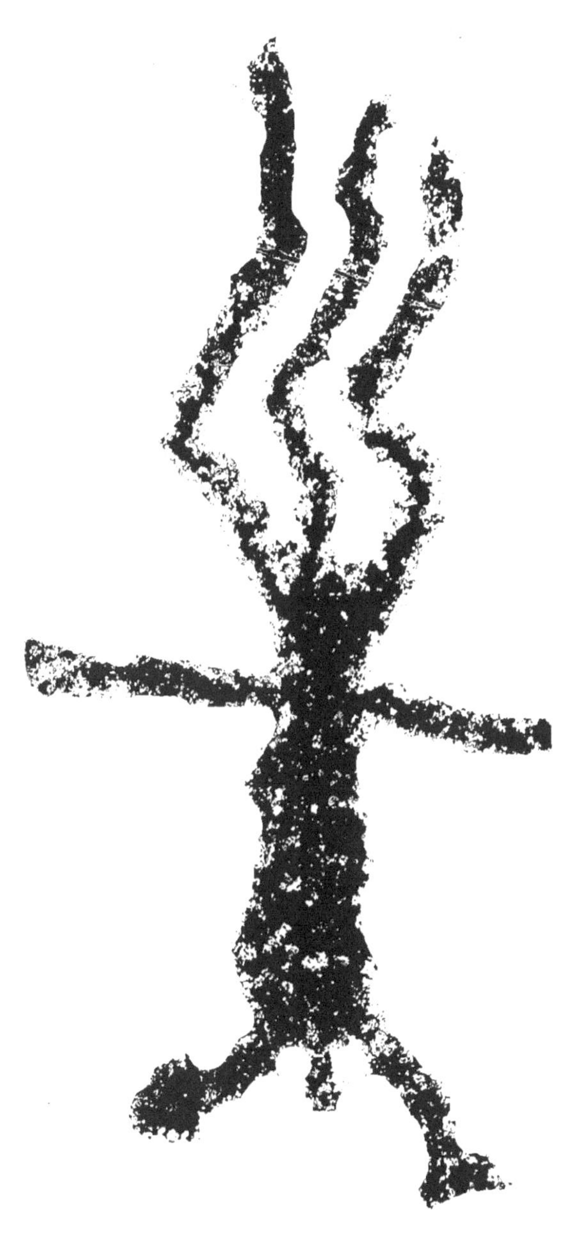

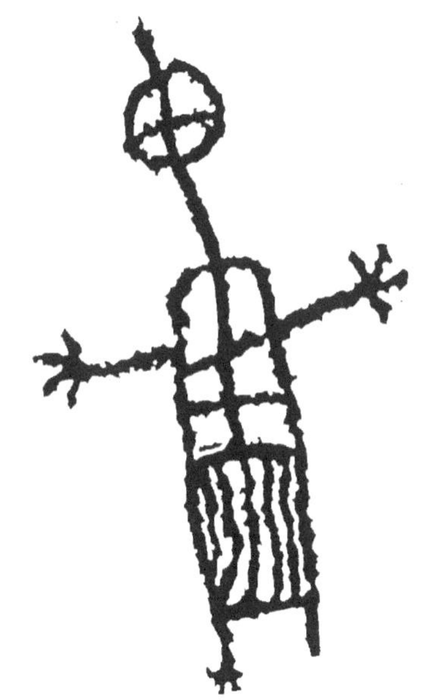

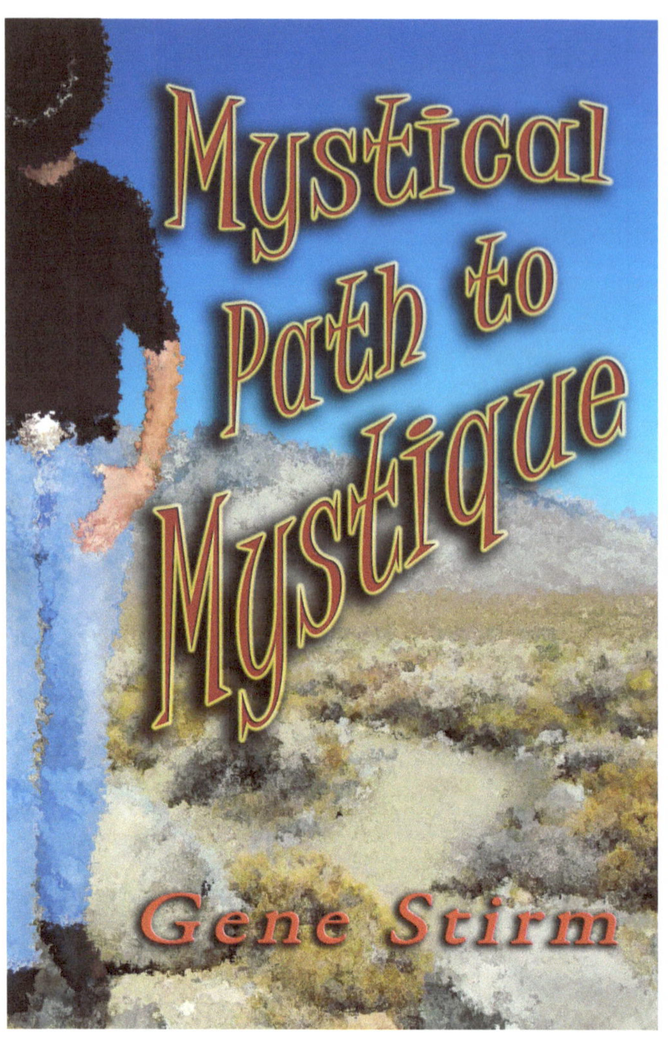

Mystical Path to Mystique

by Gene Stirm

ISBN-13:978-0-9826828-0-7

After a bump on the head, Dave, a crusty two timed divorced, ex LA ad man turned maintenance man, starts seeing a ghostly image of an American Indian reflected in windows and mirrors. When he is fired from one more menial job on his long road to wreck and ruin, he makes a choice, get out of town. So he loads all his worldly possessions into the back of his pickup truck and heads to Northern California, to a piece of land he had inherited. On the way he picks up a mysterious hitchhiker, who takes him on the journey of a lifetime where all his hidden secrets are unmasked, and he is confronted by his past, his weaknesses and his fears. Can a simple act of forgiveness and letting go, actually bring happiness and fulfillment and could the beautiful widow he met at a rest stop be his solemate, or is it all an illusion to be snatch away just when he finds hope? Find out as you join Dave on his Mystical Path to Mystique.

Trent, the hitchhiker, slowly reveals the fact that he is a Shaman and Mystic Traveler sent to help Dave find his way. However, when his own romantic involvement distracts him, he must choose between personal passionate pleasure and a higher commitment in order to save Dave's life. And what of the ghostly Indian, is it a Spirit Guide or the effects of the bump on his head?

This mystical romantic adventure makes many twists and turns on its way to Mystique.

Available in Bookstores and from Amazon.com

www.ingramcontent.com/pod-product-compliance
Lightning Source LLC
LaVergne TN
LVHW070143110826
845147LV00002B/316

* 9 7 8 0 9 8 2 6 8 2 8 2 1 *